AF413273

THE
WATSONS
of
TETHERTOWN

THE
WATSONS
of
TETHERTOWN

a novel

by

MARY HOPKINS MOORE

THE WATSONS OF TETHERTOWN

FIRST EDITION

Edited by Ellen Clair Lamb and KS Revivo.

Cover and interior designed by KS Revivo.

ISBN 979-8-218-38093-9

To Tom, who always helps make my dreams come true.

THE
WATSONS
of
TETHERTOWN

A Note from the Author

Growing up, I always enjoyed hearing my parents' stories of their parents and grandparents. I liked imagining a world of long ago before television, cars, electricity, telephones, and all the other things we take for granted. What was it like to live in a world like that?

I was especially captivated by the stories of my great grandfather on my mother's side, Joel Watson. He had a hard life. That said, he was hard working, tough, and smart—took his flailing family farm and made it a success. But along with that success, he had to weather many tragedies. Somehow, he remained positive and kind. In fact, my mother used to talk about how he would never even discipline my grandmother and her sisters because he was too softhearted. How did he survive this hard life and not become bitter? What did he do when his children fell ill but had no antibiotics or modern medicine to cure them? How did he bear the loss of life that was so commonplace back then? According to my mother and grandmother, he remained thoughtful and loving all his life.

Most of this book is fiction, including a few of the characters. I had never even met most of the "real" family members—many died before I was born, others lived too far away. But through my mother's eyes, I believe I got a sense of who they were.

Our families are the rock that helps weather the tough times and celebrate the joyous times. As I researched and composed this book I realized that it was family that sustained them through all these tragedies and hardships. Their love for each other saved them.

Today, we also can weather any storm, as long as we have people around us who support and love us.

I hope you enjoy reading this book as much as I enjoyed writing it.

Mary Hopkins Moore,
February 2024

ONE

Joel

- Summer, 1886 -

The moonlit night's beauty escaped Joel's notice. His anger coiled inside him like a snake, ready to strike.

This was it. The man—called stepfather, but "father" could not be further from the truth—had taken everything from him. Gone were his farm, his mother, his home, his peace of mind. Even all that, Joel could live with, but when he'd returned from town late that evening and saw his mother's face—well, that could not be borne. She was black and blue. Her look of terror chilled him.

His stepfather had left the house. Joel begged his mother to leave with him that evening and go to her own mother's house. She refused, partly because her mother would have most likely closed the door on her (she told her not to marry that vile man) but also because she was afraid of what her husband would do when he returned home to find her gone.

"I am sorry to say that instead, you must leave, Joel," she had told him. "Your very presence sets him off. I overheard him speaking to one of his friends last night about transferring the farm deed to his name so he could leave it to Billy. I stood up to him, as I cannot in conscience agree with his plan to rob you of your father's farm."

Anna was quiet for a moment, then sighed. "He lost his temper. Perhaps if you are gone, he will calm down and things will be better for me. But I cannot help you, not anymore. I am legally bound to him, and he can make my life very hard. Maybe you can take measures to regain the farm with your uncle's help."

Of course that was hopeless. His uncle would never go up against the powerful Bill Preston. Bill had ties to the law, judges, and controlled a group of violent men who owed him—only God knew why—and who would do whatever he asked. Joel had little hope for a legal barrier to his stepfather's plan.

If the man died before his plans were complete, the farm would be Joel's without question. His mother would be safe, and he could get on with his life.

Without thinking, Joel ran as fast as he could to his neighbor Wallace Hart's house. The family was away. Joel knew where Wallace kept his rifle.

Joel found the gun in the Harts' kitchen. He picked it up, grabbed some bullets, tore out of the Harts' house and ran down the drive.

His mind racing, he decided he would wait a way down the road and ambush his stepfather before he got too close to their farm. He would do what he had to do.

He ran across the Hart's farm, clutching the rifle with madness in his eyes. As he came to the town road, a wagon rolled toward him. On the seat of the wagon he recognized his good friend Amos's father, Mr. Fraser. He ducked his head and passed the wagon, walking quickly.

"Whoa!" the man shouted to his horses. He climbed down from the rig and called, "Joel, where are you off to in such a hurry? Come back here and speak to me, son."

Perhaps it was the word "son" that stopped Joel in his tracks—his father had called him that. Or maybe it was the note of concern he heard in Mr. Fraser's voice.

At any rate, he turned around.

Ebenezer Fraser knew of Joel's stepfather and his plan, of course. It was common knowledge, or at least suspected by a good many folks around there. He surmised that things had come to a head, and that Joel was about to ruin his life.

"Put that rifle down, Joel. Let's sit and talk for a spell."

"No sir," Joel replied in a clipped voice. "I need to protect my mother. I have stood all I can. I must go."

Joel turned and began walking quickly.

Mr. Fraser ran back to his wagon, turned it around and cut Joel off.

"Joel, come sit in the wagon for a minute," he said. "Calm down and make sure you think this through."

The tone of his voice was enough to make Joel stop. He looked at Mr. Fraser and remembered his father riding in that wagon, while Joel and Amos were in the back playing and laughing. He swallowed hard, put down the gun, and climbed up.

The two neighbors sat silently in the wagon. All around them the cicadas and the frogs were giving their nightly concert. The soft Missouri breeze lifted Joel's long hair—he had forgotten to grab a hat. A billion stars sparkled in the sky and the moon glared down at them. Coyotes howled in the distance.

"Tell me what happened," Mr. Fraser said quietly.

Joel explained it all: how his stepfather belittled him, sneered at him, even beat him, all the while praising his own son, Billy (whom Joel hated with a passion.) This he expected and had grown used to, but the violence toward his mother and plan to steal his farm had been too much. He needed to take matters into his own hands.

"How will killing this man help your mother?" Mr. Fraser asked. "They'll hang you for sure. You're almost eighteen, so a judge will consider you an adult."

"At least Ma won't suffer violence from him anymore," Joel said.

"Think, Joel. Would your mother ever recover from you being hanged? That would be so much worse for her—and you. And in the end, your stepfather and Billy would be granted the farm anyway. This solution does not make sense."

Joel covered his face. "I just can't take this. I can't lose my Pa's farm to this terrible man and his loathsome son. I cannot let my mother live a life where she is frightened all the time."

"What did your mother say?"

"She said to leave, and that Bill would calm down. She said to fight his plan legally, with the help of my uncle. But everyone knows no judge will cross him. It's hopeless. I will lose."

"Well, we won't solve this here and now. Why don't we take that rifle back to Wallace's house, and then you come to my place and stay for a while? Amos is home, and will be glad to see you. We can talk about it in the morning and come up with a plan," Mr. Fraser said.

Joel was silent. Some of his anger had cooled, but he still wanted to remove Bill from their lives forever.

"Think of what your father would want, Joel. He would never want you to throw your life away. And of course, that would break your poor mother's heart. She has enough to contend with, don't you think?"

Thinking of his father again, Joel sighed. "All right."

Mr. Fraser turned the wagon around again and they headed back to the Harts' farm.

TWO

Anna

A nna peered in the looking glass and gasped when she saw her face—a black eye and a swollen, dark bruise forming by her jaw. Her eye hurt, her face hurt, her jaw hurt. She felt sick to her stomach, and her head pounded. But worst was the feeling of betraying her son. She'd told him to leave the only home and family he had ever known. Her heart ached with sorrow and guilt.

But what else could she have done?

She'd made the mistake six years ago. A slick-talking, charming, handsome stranger had convinced her that he loved her.

She'd been desperate for help with the farm and raising a twelve-year-old boy who would need a father as he became a young man. If only Gilbert hadn't gone out in that storm all those years ago. A tree had fallen on him, and that was that.

But here she was. No use crying over her hasty decision. Really, she had only herself to blame. Her mother had been skeptical of Bill Preston, but she had not listened.

"He's too good to be true," her mother had warned.

They'd met at a church social. Anna was used to fending off advances from widowers and bachelors. Not only was she a striking looking woman with her light brown hair and arresting green eyes, but she owned a farm. Many men would love to marry Anna, but she had never been interested before.

She noticed Bill right away. He was kind and polite. One might even say he was handsome, in a rough way. He was tall with jet black hair and bright blue eyes. They struck up a conversation and spoke about her life on the farm. She talked about how she ran the farm and found herself admitting that she was not managing well. Her foreman had left to marry his sweetheart in Kansas, and she had not found anyone to replace him.

After they'd talked for some time, Bill asked if he could see her again. She demurred, mostly out of habit. That did not discourage Bill, though. The next day, he came out to the farm to see if she needed help with the chores.

Frankly, she did need help. Her two farmhands had been less than dependable since the manager left. One was as lazy as the other. More times than not, she was outside tending to the stock. Joel helped, but he was still in school and she wanted him to finish, maybe go to college someday. Things were coming to a head. She could not continue as things were.

Bill brought his son Billy to help that day as well. Billy was big and strong. He was a handsome boy with sandy colored hair and lots of freckles. But Billy didn't seem to smile much. He was the same age as Joel, but he told her that he "did not take to book-learnin" so had quit school.

At the end of the day, Anna insisted on trying to pay them for their help.

"Oh no, ma'am," protested Bill. "We're just being neighborly."

"Well, thank you kindly for your help today, but we won't be needing any more assistance. I am interviewing a farm manager tomorrow," she said primly.

Just then, Joel returned from his chores and eyed the two visitors.

"We are much obliged for your help today," he said stiffly. "But no need to come help again—I will stay home from school until we hire a new man."

"Well, sure, young man," Bill said in a respectful tone. "I am hoping, though, that this day's work earns me enough credit to ask your Ma here to accompany me to the church bazaar next week. That is, if you wouldn't mind."

Anna looked at her son and smiled.

"I reckon that's up to her," Joel said reluctantly

Over the next four months, Bill was attentive, kind, and helpful. When Joel was at school, Bill and his son Billy would come out to the farm to "pitch in." They made sure to leave when Joel arrived home from school so as not to "get in his way." Bill squired Anna to every event in town, and took her on picnics, buggy rides, and long walks.

When he proposed to Anna four months later, he promised to take care of her, love her, and do right by her son, who needed a firm hand—a father. So, on a sunny day in July, she happily married Bill Preston.

At first all was well. After the wedding, Bill and Billy moved in. Joel still had his own room, but Anna could see that he was uncomfortable around the new family members. She couldn't fret about that. Bill worked hard on the farm. He quickly took over and fired the new farm manager. With Billy's full time help and Joel's help when school was out, they got along fine. They were able to start saving money. Bill seemed happy with Anna and content with Joel.

Billy was another matter. Anna recalled several injuries—one fairly serious—that Joel had received while he was doing chores with Billy. He never said, but Anna suspected these "accidents" were done on purpose, that Billy was jealous. After all, Joel was gone to school for most of the day. When he was home, he often had to study for his exams instead of farm work, even though he was sure to finish his chores first. As for Billy, he worked on the farm all day.

After a while, Bill's attitude toward Joel began to change. He complained about the lack of help from Joel around the farm. Joel was up too late, wasting expensive oil for his light to read by. Joel had ideas to go to college, which would take money from the farm. Joel was not as strong as Billy, so could not do some of the tougher chores. He even begrudged the food Joel ate.

"You don't do much to put the food on the table, but you sure can take it off the table," he would say.

As time went on, Bill wanted another son. Much to her sorrow, Anna was not able to give him one. She had married Joel's father when she was older. Being even older now, she could not get pregnant. This was just another reason for Bill's resentment to grow.

Things came to a head a couple of years after they married. Joel's Uncle Don, his father's brother, came out for dinner one night. While there, he casually mentioned that Joel would be old enough in a few years to take over the farm.

"Of course," he said, "Gilbert had it in his will that Joel would inherit the farm upon his death, after he turns twenty-one."

Bill was silent the rest of the evening.

After Don left, things quickly escalated. When Joel excused himself to go study, Bill flew into a towering rage.

"Why am I working so hard on this farm?" he screamed. "Who am I killing myself for? Is this all for your weak and spoiled son? He hardly lifts a finger around here, yet he will take our farm?"

Anna pleaded with him—Joel would not send them off the farm. He needed them, and they would live there for a long time. There was room for everyone.

"Please don't worry about this," she begged. "We can't do anything about the will. And Joel would never ask us to leave!"

Anna still remembered the way he grabbed her, with his face pressed up to hers.

"You think he will want me here once he gets a wife? Will he want Billy? Or even you? You've played me for a fool," he spat.

After that night, everything changed. Bill left the farm most nights and went into town. Anna heard from the other wives that he was getting friendly with the sheriff, the mayor, even the judges. He also seemed to spend a lot of time with a group of rough men. The times he brought them out to the house, Anna would feed them.

After she finished serving them, Bill would tell her to go to the bedroom and wait for him there. His friends would laugh uproariously. She was humiliated.

He had changed in the bedroom as well. Gone was the tender, loving husband. Instead, he was an angry, resentful man who wanted "what he worked for all day." He was rough and dismissive.

But she had never imagined that he would do this.

He must have planned this, she thought. Was the farm the reason he married her? Was this why he had spent all that time in town with all those men? He wanted the farm for himself.

Her mother was right, Anna thought again.

"He wants you for something, but not for love," she had said. She had seen right through Bill Preston from day one. "Don't do it," her mother implored. "You'll regret it."

But Anna rarely listened to her mother. Her mother never supported anything Anna did. She'd even told Anna to sell the farm the day after Gilbert died. Anna had refused.

"You won't be able to handle the farm on your own," her mother predicted. That absolutely infuriated Anna.

Now Anna and her mother were estranged and did not speak, all because she married Bill against her mother's wishes. She would have nothing to do with her or with Joel. In fact, Anna heard that her mother planned on moving to Pennsylvania to live with her own sister. As Anna's father had died years ago, Anna was on her own.

I guess she was right, though, Anna thought. *But now what do I do?*

She heard Bill driving up in the buggy, so she quickly blew out the candle and got into bed, pretending to be asleep. Luckily, Bill left her alone.

THREE

As Joel opened his eyes to a beautiful summer morning, his heart sank.

He was in a tough spot. Thank God he hadn't shot Bill, although part of him regretted that immensely. He was fortunate to have run into Mr. Fraser.

He pictured his farm, the beautiful clapboard house, big red barn, and the fields. Those fields were like heaven to him. He could picture the grass moving in steady waves, with long heads of golden grain. He could almost feel the soft breeze and the warm sun on his shoulders. He could hear the echoes of his father and grandfather. Out there he always felt at peace. It was a sacred place to him—his family legacy. His land, his farm, his home.

"But now what?" he wondered aloud.

Joel sighed and got up. He poured water from the pitcher in the basin and washed his face and body the best he could. He went to put on his undershirt but it was pretty smelly—he would have to ask Amos to borrow one -- so he just put on his button-down shirt and pulled on his pants and suspenders. He put on his neckerchief just in case Mr. Fraser sent him outside to help Amos. His boots and hat were by the kitchen's back door, so he put on his dirty socks.

He wondered if he could ask one of the Frasers to go get his clothes from his mother. God knows he couldn't go back there. He didn't trust himself around that man.

Joel made his way to the kitchen, where Mrs. Fraser, Amos, and

Amos's sisters Sally and Mary greeted him. The girls and Amos sat eating at the big oak table, which was covered in a blue-checked cloth. Mrs. Fraser stood at the cook stove in a blue calico dress covered by her serviceable white apron, stirring something in a cast iron pan. She turned around when Joel walked in.

"Good morning, Joel. Are you hungry?" she asked.

Joel realized he hadn't eaten since noon yesterday. "Yes—starving! Thank you kindly, Mrs. Fraser."

"Oh, it's nothing. You are always more than welcome here."

After a few minutes of eating everything in sight, Joel started to feel better.

"Why are you here, though?" asked Sally. "Shouldn't you be at home doing chores?"

"Hush up, Sally," Amos said sternly. "It's none of our business."

"Well, it is if he's going to eat all of Ma's cinnamon rolls," Sally huffed. "I only got one! And why are you just wearing socks? Don't you have any boots?"

Guiltily, Joel put his third roll back on the serving plate. "I left them by the door," he explained.

"Sally! Mind your manners," her mother said, frowning. "Joel is our guest, and we are happy to let him eat as much as he wants. Now go scrape and wash the dishes."

Mary and Amos looked at Joel curiously.

"Are you alright?" Mary asked.

Before Joel could answer, Amos stood up. "Let's go outside and go see the new mare, Joel. There are too many nosy folks here."

"Joel, could you first go see Mr. Fraser in his study?" Mrs. Fraser asked. "He is waiting for you."

Amos raised his eyebrows at Joel. "What in the Sam Hill did you get yourself into? Do you want me to go in with you?" he whispered.

"No thanks," mumbled Joel. He got up and quickly made his way to the study, stomach churning. What would he do if Mr. Fraser asked him to leave? Where would he go?

CHAPTER THREE

Joel knocked and waited outside the study door until he heard Mr. Fraser's greeting. He walked into the dark shuttered room, closed the door, and sat down, hanging his head. He felt sick to his stomach. Where would he go? What would he do?

Mr. Fraser looked at him kindly from behind his desk. "How did you sleep?" he asked.

"Surprisingly well," answered Joel. He paused, not sure what to say next.

"I reckon that was God's providence sending me your way last night," Mr. Fraser said.

Joel straightened up in his chair. "Yes sir."

"Well, what do you want to do now?" Mr. Fraser asked. "You are nearly eighteen years old and a man. You are, of course, finished with school now. It looks to me like you don't have a home, money, or a living right now. What do you propose to do?"

"I want to get my farm back, sir," Joel sputtered. Until he spoke the words, Joel had not even known that was what he wanted. Now he had said it, he knew that was what he had to figure out. He had to somehow get his farm back and protect his mother.

"Why, is it truly not yours anymore?" Mr. Fraser asked. "And what of your murderous rage? Have you gotten past that?"

"I still feel very, very angry," Joel said slowly. "But no, I don't think I will go after Bill again that way. And I appreciate you saving me from making a bad decision last night, sir."

"Of course." Mr. Fraser waved his hand. "You have been put in an unjust and heartrending position. I was happy to help."

The two sat in silence for a while.

"I am not sure exactly what to do," Joel said at last.

"Well, let me think on that, son. In the meantime, why don't you join Amos? A few livestock need tending, and perhaps some physical labor can help you to think clearly later. I'll see if I can talk Mrs. Fraser into visiting your farm in a couple of days and grabbing some of your clothes. It might be good to check in on your mother anyway, and that's a good excuse."

"Yes, sir, I would appreciate that. I am worried for her. And thank you once again—for the place to stay, and for saving my life last night. I am very grateful." Joel bowed and left the room.

Oh my, thought Ebenezer Fraser. "*What a quandary. Whatever shall we do with this young man?*"

FOUR

Billy hurried down the stairs into the bright kitchen, late for his chores again. Pa was going to kill him. He could hear Anna still cooking breakfast, which was a relief. Maybe it wasn't that late after all.

He walked into the bright kitchen which was full of good smells—bacon, biscuits, and coffee. Miss Anna, as he called her, had on a calico dress and her back was to him at the cast iron stove. She turned around when he entered. Billy greeted her but then did a double take when he saw her face.

"What happened to you?" he blurted. Immediately, he wished he could take those words back. Obviously, Pa had hit her. He might have had a good reason. But probably not.

Anna did not answer his question. "You had better hurry and get out there," she said. "Your pa is already in the barn. From now on you will also do Joel's chores, as he has left the farm."

Billy's eyes grew wide. "What? Where did he go off to?"

"I am not sure," she said stiffly. "Please eat, and then go help your Pa."

Well, that's typical of Joel, Billy thought. *He goes off, leaves Pa and me with all the work while he goes have a good time somewhere else.*

By the time he got to the barn, he was seething.

"Where the heck is Joel?" he asked his father without thinking.

His father turned to him, eyes blazing. "That is none of your concern. And we will not speak his name or refer to him anymore. Especially around your ma. He has left."

She's not my ma, Billy almost said out loud. Sighing, he climbed up to the hayloft and got to work.

Up in the hayloft, his mind began to wander. He remembered his real ma. She had been a delicate and beautiful woman. Billy had adored her. He had happy memories of the three of them together—that was, until he turned six. That was the year she died in childbirth, and her baby died too.

Pa had cried all night. Billy had been confused; he did not really understand. His ma had been sick, and his little sister had died. But he thought his ma would get better.

The next morning, Billy had found his pa asleep at the kitchen table with an empty jug next to him. There was no breakfast. He could hear their cow Daisy mooing—she probably needed to be milked.

Billy had shaken him. "Pa," he'd said, "Daisy needs to be milked."

"Get your Ma to do it," his father mumbled, still drunk from the night before.

Billy had tiptoed into Ma and Pa's room. Ma was under the sheet. Even her face was covered. That was strange. He'd lifted the sheet and looked at her. Her face was stark white, and she was very still. He poked her and then put his hand on her face to wake her up. Her face was cold, and it felt funny. He pulled his hand away quickly then burst into tears.

"Stop yer bawling," Pa said from the doorway. "I forgot to tell you that your Ma is gone, along with your baby sister. Come on outside with me, I will teach you how to milk the cow."

Billy closed his eyes, remembering the confusion and sorrow of that day. Life was never really happy for him after that. There was no one to listen to him, to hold him when he cried as a young boy, or to just hug him. He had been abandoned by the only person who really loved him. It made for a sad and lonely childhood.

A year later, Pa had sold the farm and they started moving around. They went from town to town. Pa would work on a farm for a while. Billy might go to school, but usually he just helped Pa. After a while, Pa would get itchy feet and they would move to the next place.

After a few years, they'd ended up in this dull little town of Tethertown, Missouri. They got a room in town, but were quickly running out of money. Pa needed to find work.

People around them talked of homesteading out in Montana. Somehow, they had to earn enough money to supply themselves and make their way west. Pa talked about it incessantly—until that Sunday when Pa decided to go to the Presbyterian church in town. At church, Pa had noticed a pretty woman who seemed to be on her own. He'd gone over to talk to her.

Later that night, Pa talked about the "rich widow with the big farm" and how this could be even better than homesteading.

He'd clapped Billy on the back. "We'll go out there tomorrow to help her out so we can get some eyes on it," he said. "This could be the meal ticket we've been waitin' for, son."

Well, that hadn't sounded half bad to Billy. By then he was twelve and sick of moving from town to town. He dreamt of having a real home like they used to. He'd dropped out of school once he learned to read and do sums. The rest seemed like a waste of time and impossible to learn, since they kept moving anyway.

"Sure, Pa. I'll go with you and help. She sure is a pretty lady."

"Never mind about that. If this farm is what I'm hearing about, we gotta make this work. You be real nice and polite now, see? She's got a boy about your age, and it wouldn't hurt for you to be friendly to him."

"Yes sir," Billy replied.

They drove up to a big white two-story clapboard house. It had a large wraparound front porch and windows with shutters.

Bill whistled.

"It looks like a rich man's house," Billy whispered.

Pa gave him a dirty look. "None of that. You just keep your mouth shut except to say 'yes ma'am' and 'no ma'am,' you hear?"

"Yes sir," Billy replied, looking at the house with awe.

After knocking they went inside and met Mrs. Watson. She wasn't dressed up like when they had met her at church—just wore a faded cali-co dress—but she still looked good enough for Pa, he supposed. While Pa was talking to her about some chores they could do to help, Billy couldn't help but look around.

The house was very fine. It had beautiful furniture in the parlor, cut glass vases, beautiful paintings, soft and luxurious rugs, the works. There was a large mud room by the door, a huge kitchen with a hand pump next to a sink and one of those fancy cook stoves. There was even an indoor privy! Billy thought his eyes would bug out of his head.

Pa cleared his throat. "Son, Mrs. Watson asked you a question."

"Yes, ma'am?" he said quickly.

"I was wondering if you were going to attend the school in town. My son Joel says the schoolmaster is very learned and kind."

"Oh no, ma'am," Billy replied. "I don't really like no book-learnin'."

When she looked surprised, he added, "But I can read and do sums. So, I don't need no more schoolin', thank you, ma'am." He tried to smile.

Mrs. Watson frowned a little. "Well, it is kind of you and your father to come out and help me today. Anything you can do will be appreciated. My farmhands are lazy, and my son is at school all day."

They went outside. Billy swore he had never worked so hard in his life. Pa kept telling him that they needed to make a good impression. Billy worked as diligently and fast as he could.

About 3:00, a boy came riding up on a bay horse.

"Who are you?" the boy asked Billy rudely.

He tried to smile at him. "I'm Billy. My pa and I are here to help your ma out today."

Joel sniffed, threw Billy the reins and walked inside the house. He didn't even offer to help Billy put the horse in the barn! It was like he was a prince or something.

At that point, Pa realized they should go. The two went in to say goodbye. To Billy's surprise, Pa refused to take any money—which Billy thought was foolish. They needed money. Even more surprising was when Pa asked the boy if he could step out with his mother. The boy did not seem happy, but said yes.

Pa seemed pleased on the way home.

"I think they are our ticket to a better life, Billy," he said. "Now I just got to make her see how good her life could be married to me."

He looked at Billy sternly. "And you gotta win that boy over, son. Why don't you go back to school tomorrow and see if you can become friendly with him?"

Billy groaned. First of all, he hated school. He always felt stupid there. Even the little kids could read better than he could. Also, he could already tell he was not going to like that boy Joel. He was a lazy schoolboy. Billy was sure Joel would be too proud to give him the time of day, especially when Joel saw how stupid he was.

"Oh no, Pa. I don't want to compete with him on his own territory. I'll just stay out of his way. I think he might like that better anyway."

Pa frowned at him. "No, you will attend school. I could tell Mrs. Watson was disappointed in how little you care about book learning. She seems to put a great store on that, as does her boy. We both need to do our part here. You start tomorrow and be friendly to the lad."

"Yes sir," Billy sighed.

Of course, as he predicted, school was a disaster. Joel sensed something about Billy's pa and his ma, so was suspicious of Billy's friendly overtures. Joel and his friends completely ignored him.

The only exception was when Billy was asked to read aloud or answer a question in class. His slow-witted responses and faltering reading humiliated him. Joel and his friends snickered quietly so the schoolmaster would not hear. But Billy heard.

He'd started skipping school the next day. Pa was so busy trying to earn money through odd jobs so he could squire Mrs. Watson around town that he didn't even notice Billy was skipping. That was, until Pa ran into the schoolmaster in town.

He came home after that in a rage. He never even asked Billy why, just beat him black and blue.

So, Billy went back. He tried to just keep his head down and ignore everyone. After a while, he asked Pa again if he could stay home.

"That boy hates me, I don't know why," Billy said. "Me being around him all day isn't helping. Can't I just work with you?"

Pa sighed and agreed.

After a while, Billy's pa and Joel's ma got married. Billy could tell Joel was disgusted to have a brother like him, and didn't think much of his pa. Well, Billy didn't like Joel much either. He'd thought maybe they would share a room so they would get to be friendly at least, but Joel must've thrown a fit about it because they each ended up with their own rooms.

Anyhow, Billy loved being in that house. It was so nice. Miss Anna (as he called her) was always kind to him and tried to make him feel at home. Pa was thrilled to own such a successful farm, so he was always in a good mood. Joel studiously ignored him, so Billy's life was good.

But after school was out for the summer, Joel started doing more work around the farm at Pa's insistence—it was only right. Now, Billy was around Joel a lot more often. Joel was quiet and didn't say much, but Billy could tell he was sneering at him behind his back.

Also, Joel was so clumsy. He kept tripping or getting kicked by the cow, and even dropped a sledgehammer on his foot. That laid him up for two weeks—typical.

This went on for six years, more or less, until the day that Pa said Joel had left. Something must've happened the night before, but Billy had missed it. Joel's moving out must have had something to do with Miss Anna's face all black and blue—which made Billy sad. Now Pa was angry all the time.

Whatever it was, it had nothing to do with him. Except now he had twice as many chores.

FIVE

J oel walked out into the bright sunlit morning. He stopped by the old wooden swing. Looking around, a memory from a different sunny day long ago assaulted him.

As he closed his eyes, he could feel himself soaring higher and then plummeting back down. He could feel his father pushing the swing harder. It felt like flying. He could see his ma sitting with Mrs. Fraser setting out the picnic lunch. He could hear the sounds of Amos laughing and Baby Mary gurgling. He could feel the wind on his face. What he remembered most was that feeling of the family together and the security, happiness, and love and what it meant to him. It was such a powerful memory. It was one of the last true moments of joy he ever felt. He recalled the intense feeling of belonging. That was a good day.

Soon after he lost his father and the world as he knew it fell apart.

Joel sighed and walked toward the barn. Peering inside, he did not see Amos, so he walked toward the field where the Frasers kept their herd. Squinting in the sun, he could see Amos on his horse, way out in the field, watching the cattle in the bright sunlight.

Joel saddled up Blue and rode out to meet him.

"Can I give you a hand, Amos?" Joel asked.

"I reckon I could use some help," Amos replied. "One of the farmhands is off visiting some kin—his Pa is sick—and the other is busy shoeing the new mare."

The two rode side by side in silence, keeping an eye on the herd. A sudden cool breeze felt good on their faces as the day was turning out to be another scorcher. The breeze kicked up the dust—it hadn't rained in weeks- so they both pulled up their neckerchiefs.

After a while, Amos stopped his work and eyed Joel. "Well, what do you got to say for yourself?" he asked.

Joel thought a moment before answering. "My ma asked me to leave the farm," he said.

"She asked you to leave your farm? I don't understand."

Joel looked uncomfortable. "You know what Bill is like. Ma overheard him declaring his intention of cheating me out of the farm. She confronted him. It did not go well for Ma."

Amos looked at him sadly. "Well, that's a real shame, Joel. I'm not surprised, though. I thought he probably had a nefarious reason for hanging around with those judges and those low-lifes outside of town. So, what are you gonna do?"

"I dunno. I guess I'll stay here for a spell and help out if it's all right with your folks."

"I'm sure that would be fine by them. We could use the extra help on the farm. But what about school? And then what? You might need some legal help. Say, ain't your Uncle Don a lawyer?"

"Yup. But I don't reckon he'll want to get on the wrong side of Bill now that he's so friendly with the sheriff. As for school, I guess I'm done," Joel replied bleakly.

"Well, he's your pa's brother, ain't he? He won't let that injustice stand. Folks round here won't take too kindly to that man stealing your birthright."

"Maybe so, but I don't see anybody crossing him right now," Joel said glumly.

"Well, did you talk to Pa about it?" Amos asked.

"Yes. He kept me from murdering Bill in his bed last night. He's going to chaw on it." Joel sighed.

"Murdering Bill? Well, I'm glad you didn't or you'd be in jail waitin' to be hanged right now. Huh. I wondered why you were here this morning."

Amos said.

"Yup." And with that, Joel ended the conversation and the boys went back to feeding the stock.

That evening after supper, Mr. Fraser called him into his study.

"Joel, I'm thinking of going into town tomorrow to inquire about your situation with my lawyer, Jedidiah Tombs. Would that be all right with you?"

"I'd be much obliged, sir. Should I go with you?"

"No, Joel, I don't think that it would be wise for you to be seen visiting with a lawyer right now. It will get back to Bill. Perhaps you lay low, go back to school or work on my farm for a while. Of course if you work here, I will pay you."

"Thank you, sir. I do not have any income right now, so I would be grateful for the money."

"Of course, of course. Well, you can stay here in the house at night and work on the farm during the day. God knows we need the help, anyway."

"Perhaps I should move into the bunkhouse tomorrow instead. I will work hard for you. But I don't want the fellas to get the wrong idea—like I'm above them or anything."

"Yes, well perhaps you are right." Mr. Fraser paused. "I'm happy to do this for you. And for your father. He was a good friend to me all my life. It would pain him greatly to see this sad state of affairs."

Joel sighed.

"Yes, I believe it would. Thanks again, Mr. Fraser." He stood up.

"Certainly. We'll talk after I return from town. Go speak to Gordon in the bunkhouse, he'll set you up with a bed and some work for tomorrow."

Joel nodded, left the room, and walked out to the bunkhouse. It was a nice sized log cabin with a big fire in the fireplace, plenty of bunk beds, and a cookstove with an indoor pump—quite a luxury for a bunkhouse. There was a table and chairs in the center of the room where a couple of men were sitting eating their dinner.

One of the men eyed Joel.

"So, you out here with the cowboys now?" he asked.

"Yes sir," Joel answered, feeling awkward.

"Ha—I ain't no sir. Anyhow, just pick out a bunk. Where's your gear? Oh, I guess you left it at your Mama's house, huh?" The other man snickered.

Joel didn't answer but instead picked out an empty bed, took off his boots and hat, and lied down. It had been a long day.

He worked as hard as he could the next day, trying to prove that he could handle being a cowboy. Of course, the "real" cowboys worked twice as fast as he did. He had a lot to learn.

As he chased cattle and shoveled manure, Joel tried to block thoughts of his own farm out of his head. It helped to have Amos there, working side-by-side with him, cracking jokes and making him feel at home. But it was not his home. It made him sad, but he supposed he would get used to it.

The next evening when Mr. Fraser called him into his study, Joel had a sick feeling.

"Jedidiah says to wait, Joel," Mr. Fraser said kindly. "Let's see what Bill does before we respond. Maybe it's all talk. In the meantime, you just stay on here. We're happy and grateful for your help. And also, it's fine if you want to go back to school. Mrs. Fraser is having a conniption about you quitting school. And she wants you to move back into the house."

"Thank you, sir, but I would rather keep things the way they are now. I don't plan on going to college now anyhow. And I like the bunkhouse. I'll speak to Mrs. Fraser."

Joel stood up, shook Mr. Fraser's hand, and left the room. He was both relieved to have a place to live and disappointed that he would not be going home anytime soon. He would need to bide his time.

SIX

Joel

- February 1888 -

Joel and Amos jumped on their horses and took off for town. It was a beautiful winter evening. There was still snow in the fields all around them and on the road, although it was hard packed so made for easier riding. A calf had been born that morning, and they had stayed up all night with her dam. Even though they were dead tired from the long day, a night away from the farm at a church dance was just what they needed.

Times had been hard for cattle farmers the past eighteen months. During the winter of 1887, a blizzard with sixteen inches of snow and a temperature of nearly thirty-five below zero had killed the majority of the cattle in Missouri. The Frasers lost more than half of their herd. In addition, they lost some of their grazing land due to harsh winters and summer droughts and had little hay to feed their starving cattle.

Then at the beginning of January that year, another blizzard came, which killed off more cattle. Some farmers were ready to give up cattle farming and move back east.

Amos had quit school the same time Joel did. Times were tough and Amos saw he needed to pitch in. As Joel and Amos took on more of the work, Amos's pa was able to let some of the farmhands go. Amos even moved into the bunkhouse, to the chagrin of his mother. With both Amos and Joel working full time, the Frasers were able to pare down to just a couple of hands.

The young men had taken pains to prepare for the dance. They had dragged the big bathtub into the kitchen and took baths, something they usually saved for the summer. Mrs. Fraser had made a fine-looking three-piece suit for each of the young men the month before, which they wore for the first time that evening. In all their finery and with their hair slicked back, Mary and Sally teased that they were unrecognizable.

As they trotted down the road, the young men began discussing the fate of their farms.

"I got the sense last week at the Grange that Bill was struggling to make ends meet on your farm again this year," Amos said. "He lost almost all of your cattle last year. I overheard that banker fellow say something about a mortgage."

"How can he get a mortgage when I am the legal owner of the farm? Or I will be, next year," Joel said in a bitter tone.

"Well, I reckon your ma is still listed as the owner. Anyhow, things aren't going well over there. I heard Billy is just about fed up and wants to stake a claim in Montana," Amos said.

"That man is going to run my farm into the ground," Joel snapped. "I need to do something before he loses it. But what? Your pa says to wait until I am twenty-one and go to court to have it legally transferred to me. But will that work with so many in town on Bill's side?"

"I am sorry I brought it up," Amos said. "But there ain't nothing you can do about it tonight. Let's hurry into town before all the gals are taken."

They spurred their horses on and soon approached the Farmers' Grange Hall.

Amos and Joel walked into the Grange stomping their feet, with hats in hand. After removing their outerwear and placing it on the big table by the door, they looked around. The hall was almost unrecognizable. Streamers and soft candlelight made the place look festive. A banner declared this was the "Annual Winter Dance." That confused Joel a bit, as he did not remember a dance last winter. Of course, the winter that year had been very hard, bitter cold, and miserable. Ranchers had all lost cattle. And very few souls would brave those cold nights to ride into town for a dance. A person could freeze to death on their way to or from town.

The fiddle player started up a catchy tune and soon couples were out on the floor, swinging around. As Joel looked around for a familiar face, he spied a gorgeous brunette dancing with that idiot Garner Smith. He remembered Garner from school. His pa owned one of the biggest farms in Missouri, but Garner had never worked on the farm a day in his life.

Amos leaned over to Joel. "What in tarnation is Garner doing here? I thought he was at that fancy Ag college at the University."

"He flunked out is what I hear," a voice behind them said quietly. Joel and Amos turned around to see their old school pal George Hanson. "Couldn't happen to a nicer guy." George grinned.

The boys clapped each other on the back.

"Who is he dancing with?" Joel asked George.

"Oh, that is Miss Belle Hughes," George informed them. "She's visiting her cousin Missy Hughes this winter. Remember Missy, a few years ahead of us at school? Anyway, Belle's stepfather is William Westlake. He owns that big farm outside Cameron. I hear he's real strict—never lets her go anywhere—but she's getting older, so maybe he's easin' up a bit."

Joel could not take his eyes off the beautiful Belle Hughes. Just looking at her made his heart beat faster. She looked like she was having a good time with Garner—she was laughing, anyway—but he needed to go meet her. Her green silk dress spun around as she smiled charmingly at her partner. Her cheeks glowed pink and bright eyes sparkled even in the dim lighting. She sure was pretty. Joel wanted to dance with her desperately.

"Uh oh," Amos said to George. "Looks like lightning has struck our friend Joel."

The boys snickered, but Joel did not hear a word they said.

"Say, George, do you think you could introduce me to her?" Joel asked, not taking his eyes off of the beautiful girl.

"As I haven't met her yet, I don't think so," George said. "But hey, look over there! I see Missy dancing with your brother Billy. I bet if you ask her to dance, she might introduce you. She probably wants to get away from that buffoon anyway." No love was lost between Billy and most of Joel's friends.

"First of all, he is not my brother. And I really want to avoid Billy right now, so I'll wait until he leaves her for a second and go ask her." Joel said.

A couple of minutes later Billy left, supposedly to get Missy some punch. Joel made his way over to her quickly.

"Hello, Missy," Joel said casually. "How are you doing? How's your family?"

"Oh, hello Joel. Well, everyone is just fine. I would ask about yours, but since you never see them—anyway, what do you want?" she asked.

"What do you mean? I was just being friendly," Joel protested. "I was going to ask you to dance."

"No, thank you," Missy said. "I really don't want to get in between you and your brother. He's been courtin' me for a while. I don't think he would take kindly to me dancing with you, of all people. What do you really want?" she asked sharply.

"Well, first of all, I had no idea he was courting you. But since you asked, I would like to meet your cousin, if you would not mind," Joel said, smiling tentatively.

"You and every other cowboy in the room," sighed Missy. "But all right, when she gets off the floor with Garner, approach me. I'll introduce you. But I gotta warn you—there is a lot of competition for a dance with her. Three other boys have asked her already and she has refused. Not sure why she said yes to Garner." She sniffed. "Well, there's no accounting for taste."

"Much obliged, Missy," Joel said and hurried away so he had a clear view of her and of Belle.

A few minutes later, the fiddler took a break. Belle made her way over to her cousin. Joel assumed an air of nonchalance and sauntered over to them.

"Good evening, ladies, Garner," he nodded. Looking at Belle directly he added, "I don't believe I have had the pleasure of your acquaintance, Miss—"

Missy sighed. "Belle, this is Joel Watson. Joel, this is Miss Belle Hughes."

"How do you do?" Belle said primly.

"Very well, thank you, ma'am," Joel said. "How are you enjoying our little town?"

"Just fine," Belle answered.

"What exactly do you want, Joel?" Garner asked.

Joel ignored him. "I understand you are from Cameron," he said. "I hear it's a fine country for farming there."

"Well, yes. I suppose it is," Belle answered.

"Joel, Belle is otherwise engaged tonight," Garner said with a smirk. "Now that you have met her, perhaps you should move on."

Belle turned to look at Garner, frowning. Then she turned back to Joel.

"I am wondering if you know how to dance, sir?" she asked Joel. "I ask because I have not seen you on the dance floor as of yet."

Joel felt a thrill go through him. She had noticed him!

"Oh yes, ma'am. I enjoy dancing," he said. "I wonder if you would do me the honor of a turn around the floor once the fiddler returns?"

"Certainly," Belle answered. "But I would hope you would honor some of the other young ladies here with a dance as well. There seems to be a shortage of male partners tonight."

"Oh yes, of course. Perhaps once the fiddler returns, we can take a turn and then I can be free to dance with others. Right now I don't believe I could dance well with a different partner," Joel said, smiling into her eyes.

Garner started to sputter.

Missy broke in. "Garner, I wonder if you would get us some punch?" she asked.

Garner bowed to them stiffly and walked off.

"I declare, you sure riled him up Joel," Missy said. "Is there bad blood between you? Or is it just the charms of my sweet cousin that set him off?"

Joel shrugged. "I have never had a quarrel with him. Until tonight, I guess."

Belle sighed. "Perhaps we should go, Missy. I don't want to cause any trouble."

"Oh no, Miss Hughes, you must stay! Garner will be all right. He's just used to having his own way. But we can't let his behavior keep us from doing what we will," Joel said.

"Perhaps you are right, Mr. Watson. I see the fiddler is returning," Belle said, looking at the stage.

Joel bowed and held his hand out to her. "May I have the honor, Miss Hughes?"

"Certainly, sir," Belle smiled at him, dimples showing.

As Joel held Belle, he felt a sensation that he had never felt before. He was so flustered he had a hard time concentrating on his steps. Holding this young woman in his arms felt like heaven. It seemed impossible, but he felt as if he was falling in love already. He just wanted to keep holding her. But, before he knew it, their dance was over.

"May we dance again?" he asked hopefully.

"Not right now," Belle answered, looking at Garner, glowering on the side of the dance floor. "But ask me again. And go help out some of those lonely ladies by the punch bowl. Everyone deserves to dance tonight."

The night passed by in a blur for Joel. He dutifully danced with other partners, while returning to Belle as frequently as he could. Every time they danced, he felt more and more like he never wanted to let her go. Of course, Garner also had a few dances with her, along with a few other men. Too soon, the party ended.

As Garner was helping Belle with her wrap, Joel approached them. "Before you leave, I wonder if I may have a word, Miss Hughes?"

"It's getting late. Don't you have to get back to work, farmhand?" Garner spat.

"I appreciate your concern for my welfare, Garner. This will just take a moment, Miss Hughes," he replied.

"Perhaps you can walk me to my buggy, Mr. Watson," Belle suggested.

As they walked out into the crisp night, with millions of stars twinkling above them, Belle sighed.

"I appreciate you not taking the bait back there. Garner is a little too territorial for me. I am a free woman. I do not belong to any man," she said. "Although certainly my stepfather would approve of Garner. He is set to inherit one of the most profitable farms in the area."

"No, ma'am, I did not think you belonged to him. But I wonder if I may call on you in the future? I would very much like to get to know you better," Joel said.

"Is it true you are a farmhand?" Belle asked. "I ask because Garner offered that you went to school with him. That seems unusual for a poor farmhand."

"Oh yes, Miss Hughes. It's a long story, but one that I hope will have a happy conclusion once I turn twenty-one," he answered.

"Well, I look forward to hearing your story, Mr. Watson. Yes, you may call on me. Although most likely, my stepfather would not approve. However, since he is not here, what he doesn't know won't hurt him." She smiled at Joel again, and he felt yet another thrill go through him.

"Perhaps I could call on you tomorrow? It is Sunday, and my only day of rest and freedom."

"You may walk me home from church," Belle said. "Now please help me into the carriage. I can see Missy is impatient to get home. And I am sure you would like to say hello to your brother Billy before he leaves." She nodded toward her cousin and Billy.

"Oh, yes. Thank you so much, Miss Hughes." Joel helped her into the buggy.

"One more thing," she said, looking at Joel. "You may call me Belle. All my friends do."

"Yes ma'am—I mean Belle. And please call me Joel."

"All right, Joel. I look forward to seeing you at church," she said.

"I look forward to seeing you as well," Joel replied with a wide smile. "Thank you and goodnight, Belle."

Realizing that he would have to speak to Billy or Belle might wonder at his unfriendliness toward his stepbrother, Joel waited until Billy was free and approached him.

"Hello, Billy," Joel said casually. "How are you?"

Billy scowled at Joel. "What do you want?"

Joel held up his hands. "Just to say hello. How's my mother?"

"She is fine, as you would know if you ever came to see her."

"Well, that is a fine idea," Joel replied. "I don't know that your father would want to see me, though. Maybe I will look for her at church tomorrow."

"As you deserted us on the farm, I am sure my father would not want to see you. But your ma seems sad. I would think you might want to find her at church. I take it you haven't been going to church since you moved out," Billy said.

"No, I haven't. And for your information, I only left because of the violence your father did to my mother. She felt that if I were gone, he would stop. Has he?" Joel asked.

"Far as I know," Billy said in a surly tone.

Joel nodded to him and left.

On the way home, Joel tried to recapture that feeling he had with Belle in his arms, but the conversation with Billy stuck in his craw. How dare he accuse him of neglecting his ma? He was protecting her. And to do so he had to be away from his land, his home.

I gotta do something about it, he thought. Now that I am getting older, and if I want to have a future with Belle.

"You okay there? Cat got your tongue?" Amos asked.

"Yes," Joel answered. "I'm just thinking that I need to start working on getting my land back."

"I guess you are smitten with that Belle. Thinking of wedding bells already?" Amos grinned.

"Hardly. She wouldn't have me now. I got nothing to offer," Joel said darkly. "And I am sure her stepfather would not give me the time of day."

"Well, I am sure you and my pa can come up with a plan," Amos replied. "I will help if I can. You are like the brother I never had. We'll figure this out together."

"Thanks," sighed Joel. One could only hope.

SEVEN

Belle

As Missy drove their buggy home from the dance in the cold, dark night, Belle was silently thinking. What was it about that farmhand that had made her lose all reason and invite him not only to call her by her first name, but to walk her home from church the next day? Most certainly, her stepfather and mother would not have approved.

Was it just a reaction to Garner's annoying behavior? He was so possessive. She had only stepped out with him a couple of times and now he acted like he owned her. It infuriated Belle, and that was never a good thing. She had a quick temper. As always, her temper made her lose sight of reason and do something she would not have dreamed of otherwise.

"You are awfully quiet, cousin," remarked Missy. "Dreaming of Garner and his many charms?"

"Not really. Actually, I am wondering why I told Joel Watson he could walk me home from church tomorrow. Do I really want him to walk me home, or do I just want to show Garner he doesn't own me?"

Missy was quiet for a moment. "Well, I am not surprised about Garner. He was always one to want his way in everything. Usually, he gets it. As for Joel Watson, I always thought he was nice, and he may have a better future than meets the eye. Plus, he is good-looking."

"Yes, he is. He might have a better future, you say?" Belle asked curiously.

"Oh yes. Billy tells me his mother asked him to leave his farm because of the problems between Joel and his stepfather. People say Bill Preston is trying to cheat Joel out of his farm, which he is to inherit soon.

I usually don't believe gossip, but Billy has hinted about his father's plan to own the farm himself someday."

"Joel is supposed to inherit the cattle farm where his mother lives? When?" Belle asked.

"In a year or two when he turns twenty-one, according to Billy. I heard my pa talking about it once. People here don't much care for his stepfather but everyone sure liked Gilbert, his father. I hear he was a kind man. My ma said he was devoted to his wife and son. It was a shame when he was killed during that storm years ago."

"What happened?" Belle asked curiously.

"I guess a tree fell on him when he was trying to move some of his cattle from his walnut grove to the barn."

"Oh," sighed Belle. "Well, that sounds like a complicated state of affairs. I wonder if I should not have agreed to let him walk me home."

"I don't see how it can hurt," Missy mused. "Like I said, he is a good-looking man, and it may take Garner down a peg or two."

"That's true," Belle said brightly.

The next day was a typical frigid February morning. Luckily the sun shone, which always cheered Belle up, even on the coldest of days. She didn't even mind walking or riding outside in the frigid cold if it was sunny.

Both Missy and Belle had dressed warmly with heavy wool coats, fur hats, and muffs. Belle's nine-year-old half-sister Beatrice was also visiting and was proudly wearing one of Belle's old velvet bonnets. She had spent quite a bit of time preening in front of the looking glass that morning.

"Do I look like you now?" she had asked Belle. "I want to be pretty too."

"You are pretty, even without the bonnet," Belle told her. "But don't let Missy's mother hear you, she will say you are too vain. That's a sin."

"It is?" Beatrice asked in a worried tone. "Then I'll try not to be vain. But if I was as pretty as you, I could not help it."

"You are such a dear," Belle said, hugging her sister.

As the family made the short walk to the Presbyterian church, Missy stopped and waved to her beau Billy, who was walking toward them.

"Stop that unladylike waving, Missy," her mother Irene hissed. "If the young man wants to notice you, he will. And he should do so first, not you!"

"Oh, Ma. It's 1888! Women are allowed to wave at men now," Missy protested. "It's not like before the war, where girls had to hide away and just hope some man might notice her."

Her mother sniffed. "You are fast on your way to becoming a spinster, Missy. You would do well to listen to your mother. How many other ladies at your advanced age of twenty-three are still unmarried in this town? Very few, that's how many."

As they made their way into the church, Belle looked around surreptitiously for Joel. She spied him sitting alone in one of the back pews. Their eyes met and Joel grinned. Belle looked away quickly while Missy nudged her.

"Seems like you have a new admirer. He must have gotten up pretty early to do his chores and make it here by now. I haven't seen him in church since he left home. I can't wait to see how Garner reacts," she said, looking around the church.

"Sssh, Missy," Belle whispered. "Someone will hear you."

"Who is it?" Beatrice whispered loudly. "Is it another one of your beaus, Belle?"

"Hush Beatrice," Missy's mother Irene said sternly. "That is not appropriate talk for church."

Belle looked over to see Garner nodding at her. She nodded back, sat in the Hugheses' pew, and the service began.

The service was long. Preacher Harris, inspired by the gospel reading of Peter's thrice denial of Jesus, spent quite some time accusing the congregation of doing the same. The preacher was determined to make them all appreciate the consequences of such behavior—which would, of course, be hellfire and brimstone. Belle found it hard to concentrate, practically feeling the eyes of the two young men on her back.

Finally, the service ended. Belle looked around and saw Joel making his way quickly toward her. But as he got closer, an older woman waylaid him. He stopped to speak to her and in those few moments, Garner arrived at her side.

"Who is that woman speaking to Joel?" she asked Garner without thinking.

"Oh, that is Anna Preston, Joel's mother. I am sure she is begging him to return home, which he keeps refusing to do," Garner said. "He's not much of a family man, I guess."

Missy broke in. "Now Garner, don't tell tales of things you know nothing about. I am sure there is a very good reason for Joel to be at the Frasers'. None of which is our concern."

Garner looked back at Belle, smiled, and bowed. "May I walk you home today?" he asked in his most charming voice.

"Not today, Garner," another voice broke in. It was Joel, who had somehow made his way to Belle's side. "Belle has agreed to let me walk her home today."

"I find that hard to believe," Garner sputtered.

Belle smiled nervously. "Thank you for your offer, Garner. But as Joel said, I had already promised him. Perhaps next time?"

Garner glowered at Joel. "Very well," he said stiffly. "I will see you soon, Belle, Missy." He bowed and strode away.

"Uh-oh," said Beatrice, who had been watching the exchanges between the young people with big eyes.

Irene walked up and took Beatrice by the hand. "Come with us, Beatrice. Your uncle and I will take you home in the buggy. We will see you all back at the house, Missy and Belle. Don't be late, lunch will be served soon."

"I want to walk with Belle!" Beatrice cried.

"No, you come with me, child," said Irene firmly.

As they walked out of church, Billy approached Missy and the two couples began to walk home together. It was a crisp clear morning, but the sidewalks were still icy. Belle and Missy walked slowly, holding tight onto the arms of their two companions.

Belle was silent at first, not sure how to respond to Garner's drama.

"Well, that was entertaining," Billy said. "Ol' Garner is starting to get his nose outta joint. It seems he takes exception to his sweetheart being walked home by a lowly farmhand. Say, I wonder if he will challenge you to a duel next?" He sniggered.

"Garner is not my beau," Belle said firmly. "He seems to have gotten ideas beyond himself. We are friends, nothing more."

"Huh," Billy said. "Well, it does not appear that Garner is acquainted with your notion of you being just friends."

"Billy, let's talk about something else," Missy said. "What is your father's plan to combat the latest report of Texas cattle fever?" she asked.

Billy and Missy fell back a bit, discussing the cattle.

As much as he wanted to hear Billy's answer, Joel knew he had just this one chance to impress Belle.

Joel looked at Belle. "I am sorry about that scene, Belle. But now I am beginning to wonder if Garner thinks you have an understanding. Does he believe he is your intended?"

"I'm not sure," Belle answered honestly. "Certainly I have never given him that idea. But I wonder if my stepfather has. I recall him encouraging me to make Garner's acquaintance before I came here. I remember thinking that was odd, as he had never wanted me to step out with any young man before."

"How did he even know Garner?" Joel asked.

Belle's eyes opened wide as she realized that Garner's father owned a big piece of land adjacent to her family's farm. It would be an advantageous match for both families—especially as Belle was the oldest with only a younger sister, and Garner was a younger son who would not inherit his father's farm. The two families could merge the land into one big property. She shared this revelation with Joel.

He was silent for a while. "How does your mother feel about all of this?"

"She never says. But I imagine she would love for me to settle down close to her. And she would never contradict my stepfather," Belle said bleakly.

With that, they arrived at her cousin's front porch. Garner had beaten them there and was standing on the porch, talking with Missy's father.

"Perhaps I can walk you home next Sunday as well?" Joel asked. "Or would you be interested in a ride in the Frasers' new cutter later today? I can come back after supper."

"That would be lovely. I believe you promised to tell me your story." She looked at the front porch and sighed. "I suppose I must not be rude and go speak with Garner. Would you like to join us?"

"No, I don't think so, Belle. But I will be back after supper in the Fraser's cutter. Maybe we can ride over to the lake if it isn't too cold," Joel said.

"I will dress warmly, just in case." Belle looked up at him shyly. "Thank you for walking me home."

Joel nodded to Billy and Missy and made his way back to church.

Belle walked up the porch steps and forced a smile. "Hello again, Garner," she said and walked into the house, Garner following her.

EIGHT

Joel & Belle

Joel made his way back to the church where he had hitched Blue, the horse he had bought for a song from Mr. Fraser. The road was a bit slippery with all the packed down snow, but Blue trotted along confidently. Blue was a ten-year-old strong, hardworking, and energetic horse. His chestnut color and bright eyes drew Joel to him the first time he saw him. They worked well as a team, and trusted each other. Joel suspected that Mr. Fraser had sold him the horse at way below its value because he knew how much Joel loved Blue. That was typical of the kind man. Joel knew he was fortunate to have his support.

On the way back to the Frasers' farm he had a lot to think about. How could he compete with Garner's prospects? Joel had an uncertain future, very little money, and not even his own home. He was young, too—only nineteen, two whole years to go till he could inherit the farm—if he was even able to inherit the farm. That is, if Bill didn't figure out a way to take it from him before then.

Then there was his mother that morning. She had pleaded with him to come home. "I was wrong, Joel. You have been gone too long. Please come back. Let's not worry about who gets the farm right now. You should be working on your father's farm."

Seeing her sad, careworn face, he had promised to think about it.

Obviously, he needed a plan. He would speak to the Frasers today— Mr. Fraser about the farm, Mrs. Fraser for help with his courtship. Both seemed like hopeless cases. But perhaps they could help him figure this out.

As he trotted along, he heard someone riding up behind him.

Billy caught up to him and slowed his horse to a walk. "Hello, Joel," Billy said.

Joel gave him a sidelong glance. "Hello, Billy," he answered suspiciously.

"Look, Joel. I don't want any trouble. I'd just like to talk to you about coming back on the farm."

Joel was shocked. "Those are words I never thought I'd hear you say."

"Look, I know your ma came up to you at church and asked you to come back. Frankly, we are in a bit of trouble," Billy said. "We've lost a few head of cattle for various reasons and had to let our last farmhand go. Now, it's really more than Pa and I can handle, especially with his daily meetings in town."

"Well, that's too bad," Joel retorted. "You all wanted me gone. Now you want me back to do work on a farm your pa is trying to steal from me? Why would I do that?"

"For the record, I never wanted you out. But now I want out," Billy said. "I want to go homestead in Montana before they're all claimed. I hope to marry Missy and bring her out there."

Joel looked at him, amazed. "But what of the plan of you inheriting the farm after Bill takes it from me?"

"I was never in favor of that, and I resent you thinking I was," Billy snapped. "Whatever gave you the idea I was?"

"Well, I dunno," Joel said slowly. "I never heard you say anything in support of my claim to the farm, I guess."

"Why the hell would I say anything?" Billy asked. "You know Pa. He would just fly into a rage, and what good would it do? But I'm done working for him—actually working for you, as I don't think there is any way for him to legally take the farm away from you. That's what I overheard when his lawyer friend came over to supper last week. Then I heard Pa saying he wanted to sell. But he would have to get your ma's permission, as the farm is in her name now. And she won't agree to that, no matter how much he bullies her."

"Huh. Well, I guess I got a lot to think about," Joel said. "I appreciate you letting me know all this, Billy. I know I haven't been a good brother to you."

"It went both ways. I thought you were a lazy, spoiled boy," Billy said ruefully. "But everyone knows how hard you have worked on Fraser's ranch. I was wrong about you, and I won't be a party to what my father is trying to do to you anymore. As I said, I'm out. I plan to leave as soon as winter is over."

The two nodded to each other and parted ways.

After Joel checked on the cattle with Amos and ate Mrs. Fraser's delicious Sunday supper, he dressed warmly for his trip to town. He hitched Blue up to the cutter and threw in some extra wool blankets for Belle. Mildred Fraser had boiled some eggs for Joel to put in his pockets. His heavy work mittens were warm, but it was a bit of a trip back and forth from town, and frostbite was always a danger in the winter, especially later in the day.

As Joel set out at a fast trot for town, he felt hopeful for the first time in a long time. His conversations with Billy and the Frasers had helped him to finally formulate a plan. He decided that when Billy left, he would move back in. He did not know how Bill would receive him, but as Mr. Fraser pointed out, he would not have much choice—Bill would need the help.

The fact was, Joel missed his home. He had always felt such a connection to the land his grandfather had homesteaded, where he had grown up. He missed his Ma.

I'm not a boy anymore, he realized. *Bill can't bully me. That's my home. He is just a temporary caretaker.*

As he drove up to the Hughes house, Belle appeared on the porch, all bundled up.

"It's not as cold as I thought it would be," she said when Joel helped her into the cutter. "Let's go see the lake!"

Joel tucked the blanket around her and hopped in. "It will be a quick trip, as I need to get you back before dark," he said. "Are you sure?"

"Yes," Belle said. "I haven't been to the lake since last fall, and I hear it's beautiful in the winter."

"Yes, I imagine it is. I don't recall ever seeing it in the winter, so this will be a treat for us both."

Belle noticed that she felt perfectly at ease sitting next to Joel, which she had never felt in close proximity to Garner. She peered at his face. He had such kind eyes and a pleasant smile. There was something about him, but she couldn't put her finger on it. She just felt comfortable in his company. Maybe he was a little rough around the edges, but he certainly was handsome, in a rugged way.

"Now it's time for me to hear your story," Belle said as they started off.

It took the whole way to the lake before Joel finished his story. Mrs. Fraser had told him to be completely truthful with Belle. Frankly, she had said, that was his only hope. As he had no real prospects until he moved back home, this was the best course of action to get her interested in him. She told him to share with her what a strong, ambitious, and honest man he was.

"Get her on your side, rooting for you," Mildred suggested. "Women love to see their men fight hard for what they want."

So, Joel left nothing out, including how devastated he was to lose his father and then to have to leave his home. Belle was spellbound.

They stopped, gazing at the beautiful lake, frozen over with the pristine snow. The sun was near to setting, and the snow reflected the pink sky. It was truly magical.

"Oh my," Belle sighed. "Have you ever seen anything so beautiful?"

"I don't believe I have," Joel said, looking at her. "You are truly a vision."

"I was speaking of the lake!" she said, blushing. "But oh, Joel, what will you do now? What if your stepfather refuses to let you back on the farm, or finds a way to take it from you?"

"It's my land. I will stand up to him and take back what my father left me," he said firmly. "Now, we must head back before it gets dark. Do you mind going a bit faster?"

"Oh, no!" Belle replied, eyes sparkling. "Let's race back."

The rest of that winter, Joel spent his Sundays squiring Belle around the area in the Fraser's cutter—that was, when she was not in Garner's cutter. Joel and Belle also spent time chatting with Missy and Billy or playing Chinese Checkers at Missy's house. Many Sundays they went riding in Billy's father's four-person cutter. Joel usually ate midday meal at the Hughes's' on Sundays and then they went off for a ride or a walk.

The more time they spent together, the more certain Joel was that this was the girl for him. Of course, Belle was beautiful but she was also intelligent and loved to read just as much as Joel did. They decided to read the book "Ivanhoe " at the same time so they could discuss it each week. Although Joel could barely keep his eyes open at the end of each day, he kept up with the reading. They both enjoyed discussing the chivalric ways of the knights and the exciting adventures of the outlaws and witch trials.

Belle could feel herself falling for Joel. If only his finances were more stable. But as his situation stood now, she knew her parents wouldn't even consider him as a serious suitor, let alone a future husband. She tried not to worry about it but just enjoy his company. She knew one of these days their courtship would most likely come to an end.

One Sunday afternoon, Billy proposed that the two race in their cutters on the old Smith Road, which was pretty wide, long and had few curves. Missy and Belle begged to ride with them too. Of course, Missy's parents would have a fit if they knew what they were up to, so they didn't mention it to them.

The two couples trotted out to the road and when they were both lined up and ready, Belle called out "Ready, set, go!"

The two cutters flew down the road. Joel's two-person cutter was lighter than Billy's, but Billy's horse was faster than Blue, so it was a pretty even race. As they neared their designated finish line—Farmer Smith's drive to his barn—a coyote ran out in front of them. Both men were able to swerve and miss the coyote, but Joel's cutter almost tipped over, which slowed him down. Billy pulled ahead and the race was over.

"That was fun," Belle exclaimed, eyes sparkling and pink cheeks glowing. "Let's do it again!"

"No, that was dangerous. You could have tipped over and gotten hurt. My parents would kill me if they knew what we just did," Missy said.

"You're right, it was foolish," Billy admitted. "On top of that, imagine Joel thinking he could beat me!"

"I would have if not for that blasted coyote," Joel said darkly.

He turned to Belle. "Are you alright? That was a bit scary."

"Oh, I'm fine," she assured him. "It was fun! But I got this weird feeling of deja-vu or something when that coyote ran out in front of us. Anyway, I guess we better not do that again. I'm sorry you lost, Joel."

"Don't you worry," Joel said, squeezing her hand. "I'll race Billy on the way home this evening and beat him then."

"We'll see about that!" Billy said and they all laughed.

The Frasers were happy to see Joel with a plan for his future, and to see him spending so much time with Belle, but they both worried for him.

"I wonder how Belle's stepfather will feel about the two of them," Ebenezer Fraser told his wife one Sunday morning after Joel left. "I am sure he would prefer Garner over Joel any day."

"Joel says that's why she continues to step out with Garner some of the time," Mildred Fraser said. "That way her stepfather doesn't get too suspicious and make her go back home."

As the March thaw began on the plains of Missouri, Joel realized it was time to go speak to Bill and his mother. He needed to move back home. Billy had not yet told them he was leaving for Montana. Joel and Billy had decided to tell them the whole plan at once.

"That way, we both have support and a solution for the farm," Billy said. "Maybe it will go smoother and Pa won't get so riled up, then."

Joel agreed.

It was ironic that now that Billy was leaving, Joel and Billy finally had the support of each other. They had started to become friends, seeing each other at the Hughes home on Sundays.

I will really miss his friendship when he goes, Joel thought. *Who would've ever believed it?*

Belle, who was still staying in town at Missy's house, was beginning to dream of a life with Joel. These days, she could only see him on Sundays and on a rare Saturday evening—if it wasn't too cold for him to drive home at night. There were plenty of socials and parties with the other young ladies in town, which she usually enjoyed. But even at those parties, she would find herself thinking of Joel and longing to be with him.

Beatrice had gone home a few weeks earlier, so Belle spent her afternoons with Missy and Irene, working on Missy's trousseau.

"When are you going to work on your trousseau, Belle?" Missy asked one cold winter afternoon while they sewed in the parlor. "You might need it soon."

"I have most of my trousseau already finished at home," Belle answered. "I declare, Mother had me start working on that when I was eight years old. I bet she will do that with Beatrice soon too."

"I have to make so many more warm clothes for those Montana winters," Missy grumbled. "I have so many pretty lawn dresses and silky shawls. I wonder if I will ever wear them on our claim. Probably not."

"You'll go into Helena sometimes for things, though," Belle said encouragingly. "I'm sure they will have church socials just like we do."

"Are you regretting that you agreed to move there?" her mother asked worriedly.

"No," Missy said slowly. "But sometimes I worry it will be so hard out there- and lonely. I will miss you all."

"You can still say no, Missy," her mother said quietly. "It is a hard life and if you don't really want that, now is the time to back out."

"Oh no, I do want it. I mean, I want to be with Billy, no matter where we are. I just worry sometimes."

On a chilly Sunday at the end of March, Joel and Billy walked the two cousins back home from church. Billy had spent the week gathering supplies, buying a sturdy wagon, and another horse. He was ready to go.

"Today is the day?" Missy asked nervously.

"Yes, today is the day." Billy said. "Before you know it, I will finish loading up and be on my way to stake a claim for our future home. I'll return in October and we can get married—if that is agreeable to you, my dear."

Missy looked at the garnet ring shining on her finger. "Of course it is—although, I would rather go with you now. How will you do it, out there all alone?"

"I will be fine," Billy said. "As I told you, my cousin Tom has a claim somewhere near Helena. I hope to stake a claim close by."

"But what if—" Missy began.

"Shhh, now, it will be alright, my darling," Billy said softly. "You will see."

Joel looked at Billy in amazement. Missy sure had changed him. Before Missy, Billy would've bristled at being second-guessed.

But of course, love changes everything, Joel thought. *I would've most likely waited until I was twenty-one to try and move back home, but Belle has definitely changed my timeline.*

"What are you smiling about?" Belle asked.

"Oh, just how much the course of our lives has changed since spending time with the Hughes girls," he said.

As they turned the corner, they all saw the buggy in front of Missy's house.

Belle stopped in her tracks. "Oh dear, there's my stepfather," she breathed.

"I'm glad he is here. It is time for me to meet him, and your ma too," Joel said firmly.

"Yes, I suppose it is," sighed Belle.

As they approached the porch, Belle's mother came outside. "Dearest Belle, how we have missed you!" she said as they climbed up the porch stairs. "Come and give me a kiss, sweet girl!"

Joel was struck at the similarity between Belle and her mother. *So this is what she will look like in twenty years*, he thought. *I hope I am with her to see it.*

"Let's all go in, everyone," her mother said. "Your father is anxious to see you, Belle. Perhaps we can meet your friend inside." She eyed Joel with a neutral expression.

Uh-oh, Joel thought. He needed to have Belle's mother on his side. He could definitely see she was not sure about him yet.

Inside, Belle kissed her stepfather and presented Joel to her parents.

Her stepfather, William Westlake, looked at Joel with little expression. "I understand you are a farmhand over at the Fraser farm?" he asked Joel.

"My goodness, let's all sit down before you start grilling the boy, William," Missy's mother Irene said. "Can you help me get the tea together, Missy?"

They left the room, along with Billy, and the two other couples made their way to the parlor. Belle made a point of sitting next to Joel on the horsehair sofa, a point that was not lost on her parents.

The Hughes' parlor was a pleasant room. But not as nice as my parlor at home, he thought.

If only he could have met the Westlakes there! Then they would have seen that he came from quality people. They would realize that he had a bright future, and perhaps a lovely home for their daughter someday.

Joel answered William with a quick summary of his background.

"I do hope to rectify things with my family," Joel added. "Later today, in fact. But I am, of course, not sure how my stepfather will react. As I said, he hopes to get the farm transferred into his name before I turn twenty-one."

"Hmmm," William said.

"I understand Billy is your stepbrother?" Mary Westlake asked in a cheerful tone. "I'm told he is planning to stake a claim in Montana."

"Yes, ma'am," Joel said. "That may also help my chances to smooth things over with my stepfather. If Billy lives in Montana, perhaps he won't worry so much about leaving the farm to Billy."

"Well, it's all pie in the sky, isn't it?" William said.

"Oh Father, Joel is trying to regain his farm, the land his father left him. We have hopes that the right thing will happen, and he will inherit next year," Belle said.

"Belle, we need to have a discussion," William replied curtly.

That was Joel's cue. He stood up.

"It was so nice to meet you, Mr. and Mrs. Westlake," he said. "I believe I will take my leave. Belle, I will see you soon, I hope."

"Let me walk you to the door," she said, standing as well.

At the door, she whispered, "Don't worry, I will take care of them. You just concentrate on your meeting with your ma and stepfather today. When do you go?"

"I had hoped to go right from here," Joel answered.

Billy walked into the room. "I'm ready if you are," he said cheerfully. "Let's make our way. I'll meet you back at the hitching post." He hustled out the door.

"Good luck," Belle said softly. "You must let me know how it goes. Can you send me a letter? I can't wait to hear until next Sunday!"

"Billy will let Missy know right away, I'm sure. I will try and come see you one night this week. I don't know if I will be at home by then or at the Frasers, though," he said.

"I will write to you if they decide to take me home today," Belle whispered. "Will you write back?"

"You know I will. But I hope that will not happen yet."

"I don't know," she said uneasily. "I don't think that Father is too happy that I have lost interest in Garner. Not that I ever was interested. I guess Missy's mother must have told them."

"I better go. I will see you soon, I hope." Joel took her hand and squeezed it. He hustled out the door and down the street.

Sighing, Belle went slowly back into the parlor.

NINE

Belle

When she re-entered the parlor, the tea was laid out but neither Missy nor her mother were there. Belle sighed and sat down on the horsehair sofa.

Here we go, she thought.

"Belle, while Joel seems like a nice young man, we are not sure he is right for you," her mother said quietly. "We were hoping for someone with a bit more prestige."

"Someone like Garner, you mean? And why is that?" Belle snapped. "Does his father's land in Cameron have anything to do with it?"

"Keep a civil tongue in your head, Daughter," William retorted. "No one said anything about Garner. But now that you mention it, he is a fine man with good prospects. Joel may or may not have a future. We would prefer a more established young man for you."

Belle took a deep breath. "Father, while Garner may be a fine young man, he is not for me. I do not enjoy spending time with him. And I do very much like spending time with Joel. He is kind, thoughtful, polite, and ambitious. It is not his fault that his stepfather is not as loving or generous as mine is. He cannot help who his mother married. I have every faith that he will work out this situation. I know there are many in town who would like to see him take over his father's farm."

"Yet, no one has stepped in to help him with the legal side, I hear," her father said. "Bill Preston has many powerful connections and Joel may not prevail, even though it is unfair. This is too big a risk for you to stake your whole future on. Isn't that so, Mother?"

"We just worry that he is not old enough and not stable enough for you right now. And if he is unable to regain his farm, you will move to Montana like his brother," Belle's mother said, wringing her hands.

"And that would break your mother's heart, as well as your little sister's. No, this is too risky for you right now, and that is my final word on the subject," William said firmly.

Belle's eyes filled with tears.

"You understand nothing!" she sobbed and ran out of the room.

Mary got up to follow Belle, but William pulled her back down. "Now stay here, Mother. Let her cry it out. In a little while you can go in and help her to pack. We need to get her away from that young man."

"Oh, but William!" Mary cried. "I can't stand to see her unhappy. Maybe this young man will work out his family situation."

"Best not give her false hope," he said softly. "If it is meant to be, it will happen. But in the meantime, we cannot have her future resting on the shoulders of a poor farmhand."

"Of course, you're right," Mary said. "But I want her to be in love with her husband, as I was—first with her father, and then with you."

"Well, that is what we all want. She's a bit young to be getting engaged, anyway. And that Watson boy is not even twenty-one yet. Let's give it some time and see what happens."

"Yes, dear," Mary answered.

In Missy's room, Belle threw herself on the bed and cried. She knew her stepfather would be unreasonable. He was just using Belle as a pawn in his ambitious plans. It wasn't fair. She was nineteen years old! She should be able to marry whom she pleased!

Missy came in and sat on the bed.

"Sssh, Belle," she said patting her on the back. "It will all be okay. Joel and Billy will make their plan work, and with an entire farm to his name, William can't say no to you. You'll see."

"Do you really think so?" sniffed Belle, sitting up.

"Yes of course," Missy answered firmly. "Now dry your tears. I overheard your father say they were taking you back today. Maybe we should go out and make a case for you to stay another week, for the Spring dance on Saturday. We should know something about what is to happen by then."

"Will we?" Belle asked.

"Yes, and if you come out in a calm manner, they might be more willing for you to stay. Maybe you say you might be willing to give Garner another look?" Missy suggested.

"Oh, no. I could never lie to them."

"Well, you will look at him—and probably dance with him too if you are here, so it's not technically a lie." Missy giggled.

"I guess it's worth a try, anyway," Belle said, drying her eyes.

Walking back out to the sitting room, Belle put on a brave face. With Missy's help, they were able to convince her parents to let her stay one more week—but only if she promised to really spend some time with Garner, just to make sure he wasn't right for her.

"Yes, I will spend some time with him," she promised. "And thank you for letting me stay. I just bought a new dress for the dance, and would hate to waste it." She smiled tremulously.

"All right, young lady," said her stepfather in a stern voice. "We will see you next Sunday. Please be packed and ready to go after church. Your mother will stay home with your sister so I will be in a hurry to get back."

"Yes, sir. Thank you both, so much!" Belle exclaimed, and kissed them.

Well, that's a relief, she thought. *Now, I wonder how Joel and Billy are doing?*

As the young men rode up to the farm, Billy felt butterflies in his stomach. When he told them of his plans, would his father fly off the handle? Would his stepmother intervene or just stay out of it? Although he was determined to go to Montana no matter what his father said, he didn't want to leave on bad terms. He truly loved his father and stepmother, and wished them well. With Joel returning to the farm, Billy felt confident that he was not leaving them in the lurch. It was a solid plan. Hopefully, his father would see it that way.

Billy was excited about the idea of staking a claim. His whole future was bright—a claim, a wonderful girl to marry, a life that was his own. He would be an independent man with his own land and then married to the woman of his dreams. He tried to envision the 165 acres he would claim. After five years, it would be theirs forever.

He would build a claim shanty, of course, but they would have to live in Helena during the winters until he was able to insulate it, and buy his own livestock. That would take a few years of odd jobs in town, and a lot of scrimping and saving. Legally, they would have to live on the claim at least seven months of the year and make improvements.

But before he could go and build his shanty to prepare to bring Missy out, he had to tell his father. Billy hoped it would go well, but seeing the grim look on Joel's face, he knew that, most likely, it would not.

"Ok, let's stick to the plan," Billy said. "I will start by letting them know my plans to leave very soon. Then you can jump in with your offer to come take my place."

Joel nodded. The two tied up their horses and went inside.

Joel looked around. He had not been in his house for nearly two years. He had stayed away, afraid of running into Bill and setting him off. He couldn't risk his mother bearing the brunt of Bill's anger towards Joel again.

The house looked just like he remembered, as if it had been frozen in time, waiting for him to return. He felt a longing for this home he had lived in for so many years.

It feels right to be here, he thought.

Their parents were in the parlor as was usual on a Sunday afternoon, a day of rest. Billy could smell his stepmother's chicken stew and he recalled that dish was Joel's favorite Sunday meal. It was almost as if she knew Joel was coming.

The young men walked into the parlor. Joel looked around, noticing that the room was spotless. His mother was always a diligent housekeeper. But all the cleaning in the world couldn't hide the fact that the furniture was starting to look worn. He was shocked to see that the rug was practically threadbare. It was plain to see that money was tight in this home.

As he looked at Bill, he noticed how old and tired he looked. How was it possible that he had aged so much over the past two years? He almost looked unwell.

Billy called out cheerfully, "Look who I brought—the prodigal son!"

Anna cried out, jumped up from her rocking chair, and embraced Joel.

"Oh, my dear!" she said tearfully. "You are here! Isn't this just wonderful, Bill?"

They turned to look at Bill.

Slowly, Bill lowered his book. "Nice of you to finally drop by," he said sarcastically. "To what do we owe the pleasure?"

"I wonder if we could sit a spell and talk?" Billy asked.

"Why, certainly," Bill answered. "What is on your mind?"

The two young men sat down.

"Father and Miss Anna, as you know, I have been courting Missy Hughes," Billy said. "Last month we became engaged. I am afraid I took my mother's ring from your drawer, Father. I am sorry I did not ask you. But I knew that my mother and you would have wanted me to have it."

"Yes, I did notice it was gone," Bill said. "But I trusted you would tell me about it in time."

"Thank you for that," Billy responded. "Missy and I have decided to start a new life together. Our plan is for me to leave for Montana very soon and stake a claim. I will return for a short time in October before the snow flies, for our wedding and to bring Missy to our new home."

Billy paused, then went on. "Because of your generosity this year, I was able to save enough money for another horse, wagon, and supplies. I bought those this week. I need to get there before all the claims near Helena are already gone. I hear there is a constant stream of men on their way out there. I need to get going."

His father was silent.

"While I realize this puts you in a bind here on the farm, I think Joel and I have come up with a solution." Billy looked at Joel.

Joel cleared his throat. "First of all, thank you for seeing me. I realize that I have not been the best son during the last two years. But I hope that we can start anew. I would like to move back home and take over Billy's share of the work. I will forgo any wages. After all, I am due to inherit the farm next year, so I need to contribute to its coffers."

"Is that it?" Bill asked sharply.

"Yes sir," Billy answered quickly. "I realize this must all come as a shock to you—"

Bill broke in. "Oh, I knew all about your engagement and plans to move to Montana already, son. Folks in town couldn't wait to tell me all about it. I was wondering when you were going to let us know."

"Pa, I realize this may seem like I am leaving you. That is why I didn't tell you until I could come up with a solution for you all and the farm. I think it makes sense to have Joel back here at the farm he was raised on, contributing to its success. But I don't want this place for me. Missy and I don't want to live here. We want our own place. We want independence. I'm sorry if that is hard to hear."

"No, no. I understand. I remember how disappointed you were when we decided to stay in Missouri instead of going to Montana all those years ago. I suspected that someday you would go. I was hoping to have you as a partner on this farm with me. But I understand you wanting your own place," Bill said.

"Billy, I am so happy for you and Missy," Anna said. "I had hoped you would marry her. She will be a fine wife."

"Thank you, Miss Anna," Billy said.

"So, are you agreeable to having me come back and work the farm?" Joel asked. "I will do a good job, sir. I have learned to work very hard these past two years. I have also learned much from Mr. Fraser about cattle farming. But, of course, I know you have a lot to teach me as well. I will do my best to carry my share of the load."

"Will you now?" Bill replied. "But how am I to trust that you also won't leave me in the lurch again? Your brother seems to have no compunction leaving his father to run this farm on his own. You also left once already. How can I trust that you would stay?"

"Sir, as I said, this is my mother's farm, and yours by association. But soon it will be my farm. I need to work toward my own future."

"Is that right?" Bill asked. "Why did you leave before then? What has changed?"

"Bill, you know that was my fault," Anna said. "I told him to go. I thought things would be better for us with him gone. I regret that now, but I think it did help him to grow up. Joel has clearly matured. From what Mildred Fraser says, he is a proficient cowhand and efficient worker. Let's give him a chance."

Bill was silent for a few moments, thinking. The others knew better than to interrupt him when he was in that state.

Finally, Bill looked at Billy.

"While I understand your excitement to 'get going,' I must insist that you wait another year before leaving. We need you. Even with Joel's help, this is a big farm and we desperately need more hands to run it. You know that. Just because Joel is more 'mature' now, he does not know our herd like you do. No, it will not do for you to leave right now. That's my final word on the subject."

Bill looked at Joel. "As for you, I will let you move back in on a trial basis. If you are as hard working and knowledgeable as you say, we could use the help."

Billy stood up. "Father, I am sorry, but I am leaving. I have worked hard and been a good son to you and to Miss Anna. But now I want my own life. I will go upstairs and pack. I'll only take my clothing and my horse."

Billy looked at Anna. "Miss Anna, thank you for everything. You've been a good stepmother to me. I am sorry to leave on such terms, but I hope you understand."

Bill rose as well. "You dare defy me, boy?" he asked in a menacing tone. "You steal your mother's ring, the money I could barely afford to pay you and then leave us in the lurch?"

"As I said, I am sorry to leave on such terms. But I must go."

"Just get your stuff and get out of here," his pa said angrily. "I don't want to ever see you again."

Billy walked over to Miss Anna, who had begun to cry, and embraced her.

"All will be well," he whispered to her as she clung to him, weeping.

Billy shook Joel's hand. "I hope to see you again before I go but if not, I wish you the best of luck, brother. If you will come outside with me in a few minutes, I will show you what I have been working on with the cattle the last few months. Then I have to go."

Joel looked at him sadly. "I will miss you, Billy. Please write and let us know how you are doing."

Billy ran upstairs and was out the door within a few minutes. Joel met him outside and helped him pack his clothing in his saddlebags as Billy explained what had been going on with the herd. There had been a couple of cases of disease which the vet said could spread if they didn't separate the sick ones from the rest. Their milk cow Bessie was almost five and would need to be impregnated for the last time soon. They hoped she would have a female so they could replace her.

"I know I don't have to tell you that there's been a problem with all of this nasty weather," he explained. "We've lost a few head. I was reading about how building some lean-to shelters out in the pasture could help some of the cattle to survive the bitter cold. But I couldn't talk Pa into it. Maybe you will have more luck next year."

"We did that at the Frasers, so maybe he will consider it," Joel said.

"Good luck," Billy said ruefully. "Bill will calm down after a while. He just likes to be in control, and he isn't anymore."

"I noticed that he looks real tired. I'll work hard, and hopefully that will help." Joel promised.

"You're right, he hasn't been himself lately. He's been even more ornery than usual, and that's saying something."

The two men stood together, silently looking at the farm. The sun was high in the sky and felt warm on their shoulders, like a promise of summer that was to come. A gust kicked up and they saw the brittle Indian grass swaying in the wind. The breeze carried the sound of the herd to them —- mooing and bawling in the hard packed field, waiting for their dinner.

"This was a good home for me for a long time," Billy said quietly. "Before this my pa and I were just wanderers. I am grateful for my years here. I have loved this land and the animals like they were my own, "

He turned to Joel. "I leave here knowing it is in good hands. After all, it was never really mine, it was always yours."

"I am grateful to you for taking care of my farm, and for watching out for my mother. It is hard to see you go, Billy. We missed so many years where we could have been friends and brothers, and I regret that now."

"I do too. But it all worked out in the end, or will as soon as you turn twenty-one."

"I hope so. I'm sure it will be uncomfortable around Bill for a while, but I'll make it work," Joel said. "Good luck-- I hope you find a good claim. I envy you. I've always wanted to go out west. Write and tell me all about it."

"I will. And I'll see you in October when I come back for Missy. Her folks have decided to give us train tickets when we go back as a wedding gift. I'll have to figure out how to buy a ticket to come back for my wedding. I spent a lot on the wagon and supplies."

"How much is a ticket? Maybe I can talk Bill into sending you the money when it gets closer."

Billy shook his head. "Ha! I doubt you'd have success with that. A train ticket is about $20 to Helena. And in case you haven't noticed, Bill tends to hold a grudge."

"Well, I'll try anyway. Farewell, brother, I wish you all the luck in the world."

The step-brothers shook hands again and Joel watched Billy ride away.

As Billy left the farm that had been his home for the past six years, he felt downhearted. He did not like the way he had left his father. Of course, he was not surprised. Bill was used to having his way and could not tolerate anyone else's opinions or decisions if they opposed his own.

Joel would figure it out, though. Luckily, from what he had heard from a friend in town, Bill's plan to take Joel's farm had come to nothing. The will had been airtight, thank goodness. And his father would still have a livelihood, working on the farm with Joel.

He did worry about how he would react when Joel inherited the farm. Who would run the farm? Would his pa be willing to step aside? He doubted it. Thank goodness he would not have to be involved with that.

Good luck to them, Billy mused. *I hope they can come to a peaceable agreement.*

But if not, he could do no more. It was time to live his own life.

As he rode up to Missy's house, she ran out on the porch. He jumped off his horse and joyfully ran to embrace his future wife and their new life.

ELEVEN

Joel

While Joel trotted along the road to meet Amos Fraser, he thought about the past week.

So much had happened. Billy left home and was already on his way to Montana. Joel had ridden over to the Frasers' Sunday night to thank them and grab his belongings from the bunkhouse. While there, he made plans with Amos to ride together to the Spring Dance that Saturday, the last day Belle would be in town. He spoke to Mr. Fraser, who confirmed what Billy had told him about Bill's inability to take his farm legally.

He busted his tail all week on the farm. He thought he did a good job—he must have, because Bill did not complain about him. It was a bit tense being around Bill, but he hoped that would change in time.

His mother was certainly happy to have him back. Her eyes shone every time she looked at him. She tried hard to smooth things over between Bill and him, but Bill just would not engage in conversation at the table, except to give orders about what they needed to accomplish the next day. That was actually fine by Joel.

What wasn't fine was the farm's financial issues. They had lost quite a few head of cattle during the blizzard the previous winter. The drought the following summer had killed a few as well. Because of the drought, the grass did not grow, so they had to use up a lot of their winter hay. Bill had to purchase more hay at the beginning of the winter as he used so much of it during the drought, which cost a fortune. It was not a good situation.

I need to figure out how to get the farm back into better shape, Joel thought. They needed to come up with a plan, or they were going to face ruin. But what to do? Even if he had ideas, most likely Bill would not listen to him. Would he have to wait until he was twenty-one to try and save his farm? He hoped not.

He also needed his farm to be in good shape if he was going to convince Belle's stepfather that he was a worthy husband. They would have to wait until he owned the farm before he could even propose. One and a half years felt like a long time. What if someone came along and swept Belle off her feet? There were a few ranchers and professional men in town, and some were quite wealthy. Like Garner.

Joel was still a boy, at least in the eyes of the law and probably in Mr. Westlake's eyes as well. He needed to figure out how to keep Belle interested in him. Just writing letters was not going to be enough. She was too beautiful, too eligible.

Again, he decided to turn to the Frasers for advice—for both the farm and his courtship. He resolved that he would ride over and see them the next day, after he walked Belle home from church.

As Amos and Joel walked into the Grange Hall, Joel spotted Belle on the dance floor, spinning around the room with Garner. Her bright blue dress twirled and shone in the dim candlelight. Even from a distance, he could see her rosy cheeks and sparkling eyes. His heart sped up, just looking at her. He badly needed to dance with her so he could touch her and be close to her.

He started to walk toward them, but Amos held him back.

"Let her finish the dance with Garner. Why don't you go ask Missy to take a turn instead?" he suggested. "I am sure Belle would be glad to see her out on the dance floor."

Amos had a point. Perhaps he needed to seem a little less eager. Maybe it even reeked of desperation at times? Should he also dance with some of the other girls? It would not hurt to let Belle see him as attractive to other girls as well. He said as much to Amos.

"That is an idea," Amos said. "But you don't want to overdo it and have her dance with Garner too much. Anyway, the song is over. She is coming this way."

When he saw Belle with her shining face walking toward him, all thoughts of dancing with another flew out of his head. She was gorgeous in the bright satin dress with large puff sleeves, her loosely-coiled auburn hair shining in the candlelight. Belle's luscious lips were turned up in a smile and her dimples were showing. He only wanted to hold one girl in his arms—the beautiful Belle Hughes. He wanted her so much it hurt.

Amos nudged Joel. "I guess I'll go find a gal to dance with. But Joel, don't forget to dance with Missy. That will impress Belle more than seeing you dance with some of these other girls."

Joel barely heard Amos as Belle approached him. The look of joy on her face was all he needed to see. They clasped hands and made their way out to the dance floor without a word.

Holding her in his arms, Joel knew for certain that all he wanted was to be with her. When he looked into her eyes, he thought he could see a spark of desire for him as well. Or at least he hoped he did, but perhaps it was just wishful thinking. After all, she was still just an innocent girl in many ways. He would need to work harder to woo her, and help her to want him too.

But not tonight. She was leaving the next day. When she danced with another young man, Joel walked outside to cool off. She was not yet ready for what he dreamed of with her. He would need to wait.

As they danced the evening away, they spoke of Joel's return to his farm and of Belle's sadness about leaving town.

"I hope Pa will let me come back soon," she said wistfully. "Missy could use more help finishing her trousseau, and perhaps I can use that as an excuse."

"What if I rode out to your place to visit on some Sundays?" Joel suggested. "I know we don't want to overdo this yet, but I feel sure Garner will be out there quite often. Would you permit me to call on you at home?"

"Of course!" Belle said happily. "But you are right about not spooking my pa. In the past there were suitors he refused to let me see. I also worry that it takes practically all day to ride to Cameron from here. Of course,

Garner will be calling on me—he does not work all week and he does have a shanty on his land out there."

"I can just get up early and ride to you," Joel assured her. "I could always stay overnight with my friend George Larue in Cameron if I need to."

"I will make arrangements for you to visit after a couple of weeks, or whenever you tell me you can come," Belle promised.

The evening ended all too soon for Joel. As he helped Belle into her cousin's buggy, he asked to walk her home from church the next day.

"My pa arrived tonight at Missy's house, so we will probably leave early tomorrow morning. I will try and talk him into letting me go to church, but he will want to get back."

"So this is goodbye?" Joel asked.

"For now," Belle said sadly. "I will write to you as soon as I get home, and every day thereafter."

"I can't promise to write every day," Joel said with a smile. "But I will write as often as I can. And I will think of you every day." He reached up and squeezed her hand. "Goodbye and take care of yourself." On impulse, he kissed her hand.

"Goodbye, Joel," Belle whispered.

. . .

The next day Joel took the buggy and drove his mother to church, just in case Belle was able to attend. To his sorrow, she was not there.

After church, Joel drove his mother home and then made his way to the Frasers' farm on Blue. He needed advice about the farm and about Belle.

The Frasers were just sitting down to Sunday afternoon dinner in their cozy dining room as he arrived. He was happy to sit with the noisy rambunctious family. After so much silence at his mother's dinner table, it was a welcome change.

It looked like Mrs. Fraser had been cooking all day. There was a big roast with potatoes, brown gravy, and biscuits with strawberry preserves she had canned the previous summer. Joel sat in his regular seat next to

Amos and after the prayer of thanksgiving, they all dug into the delicious food without hesitation.

Of course, the Fraser girls could not resist teasing him about Belle. "Are you going to marry her?" Mary asked.

"Have you kissed her yet?" Sally asked him.

Amos burst out laughing. Joel was not sure what to say. No, he had not kissed Belle Hughes yet, and that probably would not happen until they were engaged—a long time from now. He felt a bit awkward.

"Sally and Mary!" exclaimed Mildred Fraser. "Those are very rude and improper questions. Apologize to Joel at once!"

"Sorry, Joel," the girls said insincerely.

"But have you?" Sally asked again.

"All right, young lady, that is enough," Mr. Fraser said sternly. He looked at Joel. "Did you want to discuss something with me, Joel?"

"Yes, sir. If I could, after dinner, I'd be much obliged. And I would like to speak to you as well, Mrs. Fraser."

"Of course, Joel," she answered, smiling at him.

After the delicious supper, Mrs. Fraser tasked the girls with doing the dishes and she took a walk outside with Joel. The day had warmed considerably and spring was in the air.

Mrs. Fraser listened carefully to Joel's plan of writing and occasionally visiting Belle, whenever possible.

"You don't want to seem too eager, though," she advised. "Her stepfather may not like that. And don't worry about Garner. It does not seem like she really wants him to court her, no matter what her parents wish."

After a nice stroll to the barn to check on the milk cow with Mrs. Fraser, Joel went inside to find Mr. Fraser in his study. The conversation with Mr. Fraser was disheartening.

"These are tough times, Joel. We all just need to tighten our belts and get through them. If I come up with a brilliant plan, I will let you know. But frankly, there is not much we can do about disease and bad weather. I am going to plant more alfalfa for winter hay next year. I would assume you and Bill would do the same."

Joel would have to discuss that with Bill, but he knew he had to tread lightly.

I will just need to work hard and try to get along better with Bill, he thought. *Then maybe I can suggest planting more hay.*

When he returned to the farm, Sunday dinner was over and his mother and Bill were in the parlor. He decided to sit in there with them, and write to Belle. Perhaps if he spent more leisure time around Bill, he would warm up to him.

One can always hope, he thought. He sighed and entered the parlor.

TWELVE

Belle

- April, 1889 -

Dear Joel,

How long it seems since I have seen you! Was it only three weeks ago you came to my house on a Sunday afternoon in your buggy?

We had wonderful news about Billy and Missy—she is in the "family way." Missy already had names picked out! She will deliver in August. She says Billy is thrilled.

I know you must be so tired, having to carry the load of work on the ranch with Bill feeling so poorly. Did he ever go to a doctor? You did not mention that in your last letter.

Garner has been working on the shanty on his father's land, trying to make it more livable. I have given him no encouragement. But he keeps coming to call, hoping I will change my mind. But how could I do that when I care deeply for another? (You, of course!) I am sure my stepfather encourages him, but I am happy to say I believe my mother now sees that I care only for you. Above all, she wants only my happiness.

Now that spring is here, I hope to come to Tethertown for a visit soon. I could ask Pa if he would bring me to the spring dance in two weeks. My mother may come with me to help Aunt Irene sew some baby clothes to send for Missy's baby. Perhaps Pa will let me come to Tethertown if he knows Garner will be there as well. He just cannot seem to let go of that plan of Garner and me consolidating the land. However, I have hopes that by the time I am twenty-one next year, he will be ready to let me choose my life and my husband.

I must go help Mother with supper, so I will say goodbye for now.

Take care, dear Joel!
Until we meet again,
Belle

Dear Belle,

I read your letter from Tuesday with much happiness. I hope very much that you can come to visit your aunt. That would make this poor lonely cowboy very happy. With all the work on the farm, I cannot see how I could even take a Sunday to ride to Cameron. But I would love to squire you to the Spring Dance, if you will permit me to do so.

Bill is getting sicker by the day, so much so that I have had to hire a new farmhand to help me as he cannot do any work anymore. Ma finally sent for the doctor (against his wishes) and he said Bill is mighty ill. He believes he has a cancer of the lungs. At first we thought it was consumption, but the doctor said no. He will not recover.

I do dread what this will mean for Ma and for him the next months to come. The doctor said he will be in agony before he passes, but he will give us morphine to help ease the pain. He believes it will only be a matter of months. Ma is very distraught. I also feel such pity for this man, even though he was not the best stepfather to me. I cannot say I will miss him, but no one should have to suffer and die like this.

Ma has written to Billy to let him know. We have not heard from Billy since Bill refused to attend his wedding last year. At least he sent Billy a train ticket to come back for the wedding after Ma begged him to. But I guess Billy just can't seem to forgive him for not attending his wedding. I think Bill regrets that now. Hearing about a future grandchild was a wonderful bit of news to share with the poor man. It made him smile, which is a rare occurrence these days.

Darling Belle, I hope and pray that you can come to Tethertown soon. My life is so lonely without you. Only a few more months and I will inherit the farm and ask you to be my wife. We will live on the farm with my mother, and she will be good to us both. If the Lord blesses us with children, she will be a great help.

I hope and pray we do not have another drought this summer. My herd is dwindling. But no matter what may come, I will make this farm a success for our future. No matter what it takes, my dearest.

Most faithfully yours,

Joel

. . .

Joel felt the familiar thrill as he pulled up in front of the Hughes house to pick up Belle for the Spring Dance. In just a moment, he would be with Belle again. For the first time, he was to escort her to the dance in his own buggy.

Amos waved and rode off to the town hall as Joel walked up the porch steps. He removed his hat and knocked on the door. Belle's Aunt Irene came to the door and welcomed him in. Once inside, he greeted Belle's mother, and sat down.

"Belle will be out soon," her mother said.

"Yes, ma'am," Joel answered, smiling nervously. He wanted so badly to make a good impression on Belle's mother. Luckily, his mother had altered and cleaned his best suit to fit him. His body had filled out with all the farm work and his good suit hadn't fit him for quite some time. He hoped Belle's mother would notice that he dressed more as a gentleman instead of a farmhand.

If they could get Belle's mother on their side, they would have a much better chance of success in gaining Belle's stepfather's blessing. She was the key.

"And how is your farm?" her mother asked. "I understand you are running it on your own now."

"Oh yes, ma'am," Joel replied. "My stepfather is quite ill. I have hired a new farmhand to help, but it is challenging. That said, I have high hopes of a good summer and year ahead. I hope to purchase more cattle by next year."

"Oh my," Mary Westlake said. "William says we may have another drought this summer. I hope we can all survive such a difficult trial. These are hard times."

"Yes, ma'am," Joel replied. "I do have my good friend Mr. Fraser as an advisor. We have a few ideas to help keep our cattle farms going. We survived the terrible winter of 1887, so we are cautiously optimistic."

"William also says cattle prices are still too low," Mrs. Westlake said.

"Mother, I hope you are not boring Joel with Pa's bleak predictions!" Belle exclaimed walking into the parlor.

"Just being truthful," her mother replied.

Belle looked at Joel, eyes shining. "Hello, Joel," she said.

Joel jumped up and took her hand. "Hello, Belle," he said happily.

"Well, you young people run along. Please bring my daughter straight home from the dance, Joel."

"Yes, ma'am. And thank you for permitting me to escort her there."

The couple walked out into the beautiful spring night and climbed into Joel's buggy. The two made quite an elegant pair with Belle in her yellow silk dress and new feathered hat and Joel in his best suit. It was a warmish evening, so Belle only wore a shawl instead of her bulky winter coat. As they rode toward the Grange Hall, Belle said impulsively, "Let's ride over to the park and watch the sunset first. We have all night to dance."

Joel smiled at her. "I will gladly do so. The more time I have with you alone, the better."

Joel put his arm around the top of the back of the buggy seat. He was not exactly hugging Belle, but his shoulder was touching her back. She shrugged it off and he smiled ruefully at her, moving his arm back to his side.

She looked at him timidly. "My pa would not like to hear of me riding in a buggy being hugged by a suitor," she said.

"That's probably true," Joel agreed.

As they sat in the buggy watching the sunset, Joel took Belle's hand. There was a soft breeze and the setting sun gave a warm orange tinge to the sky. It was a spectacular sight.

"It's so beautiful," Belle sighed.

"Yes, you are," Joel said, looking at her face.

"I meant the sunset!" Belle retorted, blushing at the compliment. "You always do that."

"What? Just tell you what I think? You are so beautiful. I have missed you so much, my sweet Belle."

"Let's change the subject or I might get a big head," she said.

"I doubt that but all right. How long will they let you stay in town?" Joel asked. "For a few weeks, I hope?"

"Only for about two weeks," Belle answered. "Ma needs to get back. I offered to stay with my aunt to help with more of the sewing, but they won't hear of it."

"I just don't know how often I can leave the farm to come see you, " Joel said sadly. "I am even having to work on Sundays as there is so much to do, even with our new farmhand."

"I wish I could help you," she answered. "I could milk the cow and take care of the chickens. I know your ma is unable to do so, as she is caring for your stepfather."

"Sometimes I think we should marry sooner rather than later. What are we waiting for? The farm is mine now, in all but name and I'll formally inherit next October. I want us to be together. Do you think it would be possible?" Joel asked hopefully.

"I don't know," she answered truthfully. "Pa seems to be softening a bit, and I am starting to see that my mother is accepting of us. So perhaps you could approach him?"

"Oh Belle, I would like nothing better. But I don't know if he will think I am in a strong enough financial position to marry you."

"You could be right. But he could also see how serious we really are. My mother might be able to get him to relent. And I don't want to wait any longer, either," she replied, looking up at him shyly.

"When he returns to bring you home, I will speak with him," Joel said.

The two looked at each other, eyes shining.

"Let's go to the dance so I can hold you in my arms without creating a scandal," Joel grinned.

The dance was over much too quickly. Belle had to force herself to dance with Garner once, but refused any other offers. As Joel drove her home, they discussed how Joel should approach her father.

"I will be confident while being humble," he declared. "I will convince him that we will make a success of my farm, and that I will take care of you and our children too, someday. How can he say no when he sees how much I love you?"

Tears filled her eyes. "Oh, I am so happy," Belle said.

Too soon they arrived at the Hughes' house. After Joel helped her out of the buggy, Belle turned to him.

"You may kiss me," she said softly. And after they shared their first kiss, Belle went inside.

Joel drove back home, his heart full.

THIRTEEN

Joel

Joel hurried through his chores the next morning. He needed to make haste if he was going to make it to church in time to walk Belle home. Her aunt had invited him to afternoon dinner, and he planned to take her for a buggy ride afterward. As he had to be back for more chores before sundown, he had no time to waste.

Ma was busy with Bill, who was all of a sudden in a bad way. He was having trouble breathing and seemed to be in a lot of pain. Even though the doctor had said he could live for months, Joel and Anna were starting to hope he would not last much longer, as he was suffering terribly.

Billy had written to his father once he got the letter from Anna. He shared his excitement about becoming a father the next summer and expressed sorrow for his father's condition. He promised to write more, but he could not leave his claim to come say goodbye.

Joel finished the farm chores and arrived at Sunday services just in time. Sitting in the back, he was able to see Garner looking toward Belle frequently. He was sure Garner would try and take Belle on a ride in his brand-new roadster buggy. Joel would need to move fast after services to get to her in time.

The minute the congregation said "Amen," Joel was out of the pew, moving toward Belle. He reached Belle and her mother just as Garner did.

"Hello, gentlemen," Belle's mother said. "Come to walk us home?"

"Oh, yes ma'am." Joel held out his arm to Belle's mother. "Will you do me the honor if Garner is willing to walk with your lovely daughter?" he asked, smiling.

"How about a ride in my new buggy instead?" Garner asked Belle.

"No thank you, but you may walk me home," she replied. She shot Joel a grateful look, then sighed and took Garner's arm. Belle had told Joel the night before that she would be firm with Garner and let him know where her affections truly lay. Joel hoped it worked this time.

As Mary Westlake and Joel walked home together, they talked of Bill and his illness, and of Joel's mother who was tending him.

"I will come out to your farm to help her tomorrow if you think that would be acceptable," she suggested. "I am sure she could use a respite. And I would love to see your farm as well. Perhaps you can show both Belle and me around?"

Oh, thought Joel. *She wants to check out the farm to see if it is acceptable for her daughter to live on someday. How clever!*

"That would be so kind," Joel answered. "I will let my mother know, and perhaps you can eat the afternoon meal with us? She would so enjoy seeing you and Belle, I am sure."

"Oh no," replied Mary. "I would not want her to go to any trouble. She has enough to contend with."

"My stepfather sleeps a lot in the afternoon and she makes our afternoon and evening meals then, so it's no trouble," Joel assured her. "We have a farmhand who eats at our table in the afternoon as well, you know."

"Well, all right. But I will bring some food with me as well. Have folks been helping out in that way?"

"Some do, especially Mrs. Fraser," Joel answered. "But of course, we could always use more help. I'm sure my mother in particular would appreciate it."

"Hmm. Well, I will be happy to assess the situation and see if my sister-in-law and I can activate more help for your mother in the town. Perhaps that is why I am here after all. I thought it was to help sew more clothes for Missy's new baby's layette, but now I am realizing a greater need in front of me," she said.

Joel was speechless. He was so touched by her willingness to help them. *What a kind lady she is,* he thought.

"Thank you very much. I am so grateful for the thought of more help for my mother. She is having a hard time with it all. I can now see where Belle gets her sweet and generous nature from."

As they approached the house, Belle and Garner caught up with them. Her mother turned to Belle.

"Belle, why didn't you tell me how ill Joel's stepfather was? His mother has no one to help her with the household chores as well as cooking and tending to Bill. We need to see about her getting some help." With that she strode into the house, calling to her sister-in-law.

"There she goes," laughed Belle, rolling her eyes. "Your mother will have more help than she needs now!"

Belle turned to Garner. "Garner, thank you for walking me home. I hope we can stay friends."

"Of course," Garner answered stiffly. He bowed and walked away.

FOURTEEN

Belle

Belle, her aunt, and her mother got up early the next morning to cook. They made a custard pie, potato salad, fried chicken, and biscuits. Her aunt decided to come out to the farm to help as well.

After helping with the cooking, Belle hurried back to her room to dress carefully for her visit to Joel's farm. She decided to wear one of her favorite walking suits. After changing into a clean chemise and drawers, she first put on her stockings and shoes. As usual, she needed help getting dressed so her aunt's maid Eugenia came in and helped her tighten and fasten the corset. Next, she put on the corset cover and bustle pad. Eugenia helped her to put on three petticoats and then attached the sleeve supports to fill out the leg-o-mutton sleeves of her bodice. After that, Eugenia had to fasten the many buttons on the back of her bodice. Belle pulled her skirt over her head and then added her favorite red neck bow with a matching belt, also with a small bow. She pulled on her brown kid gloves.

The April weather had turned chilly that morning. For the ride out to Joel's farm, she put on her warm wool coat, thick velvet bonnet and carried her fur muff.

The Hughes' stable boy drove the ladies out to the farm and they arrived by noon. Belle was astounded when she saw the beautiful clapboard house. Yes, it could use a new coat of paint and some other touches, but clearly this was a very fine home.

As they walked up on the porch, Anna met them at the door.

"Welcome Mary, Irene, and Belle!" Anna said enthusiastically. "It's so good to see you all again. I am honored that you came all the way out here to visit us. Please come in and sit in the parlor while we wait for Joel to have a break from his work.”

“We have missed you at church,” Irene said sitting down. “But I understand you have been busy taking care of your husband. Mr. Hughes and I were sorry to hear of his illness.”

As they sat down, Belle’s mother surreptitiously took in the parlor. The room was clean, although she could not imagine how Anna had time to clean it with all the work she now had. The furnishings were old and worn, but of good quality. The rugs were threadbare, but of course these tough times meant little money left over for luxuries such as new furnishings. She was satisfied that this had once been a fine house and would be again someday, once hard times were over.

The women talked of Bill and a plan to get Anna more help. They also spoke of Billy and Missy and the upcoming birth of the baby.

After a while, Anna rose. “I need to get afternoon dinner together for us all, but please stay and relax. It won’t take me long.”

“Instead, why don’t you and I go check on Bill?” suggested Irene. “I took care of my father when he had cancer, and I might have a few ideas to help make him more comfortable.”

“That would be so kind,” Anna replied. “But I must get dinner for the men.”

“Don’t you worry about dinner. We brought it with us! Please just go check on your husband while we put it together,” Belle’s mother Mary said, smiling at Anna.

Irene had a few suggestions for taking care of Bill. Belle and her mother put the meal together. Soon Joel and the farmhand came in.

The group sat down to a wonderful meal of fried chicken, potatoes, and biscuits. The women talked about the farm as well as what kind of help Anna might need. Joel just silently ate the delicious food, not taking his eyes off Belle. She noticed and smiled at him, blushing.

“I think I can manage most of the time,” Anna said when Irene asked how they could be of assistance.

“You do need more help, ” Irene said firmly. “I’ll get the Presbyterian

Church Ladies Club to start coming out, bringing meals, and helping with some of the housework. Taking care of a dying man is a full-time job."

"We would be so grateful," Joel said quickly. "Now I have a few minutes before I need to go back out to check on the cattle. May I show you around the farm, ladies?"

"Oh no, we will stay here and help with some household chores if that is all right with you, Anna." Belle's mother answered. "But why don't you show Belle around a bit?"

After he showed Belle the rest of the house, including the five upstairs bedrooms, the couple took a quick tour around the barn. Next, they walked to look out at the pasture where he kept the cattle.

"Oh Joel, your house and farm are beautiful!" Belle exclaimed.

"Thank you. But the parlor is looking a bit worn," he said ruefully. "Maybe someday you can pick out a new rug and chairs for it. After all, it will be your home too, I hope." He smiled down at her.

"I hope so too," she said.

Belle accompanied her mother and Irene whenever they went out to the farm to help Anna. In doing so, she got to know Anna better and of course, spend more time with Joel. A few times they snuck into the barn and kissed. Belle was beginning to understand that what she was feeling for Joel went beyond just love –- it was a burning desire. She just wanted to be with him, feeling his arms around her, his mouth on hers. She wanted him. What all that would entail she was not sure. But there was no doubt in her mind that she would not be happy until they were truly together. For that, they would need to be married.

Two weeks later, Belle and her mother received a letter from William letting them know he would be there Saturday night and then take them home Sunday. Their time in Tethertown was coming to an end.

The next day, Belle went out to Joel's farm with her mother to cook and to help Anna—and to see Joel again. She needed to tell him to come see her father on Sunday morning. This would be Joel's chance to ask for Belle's hand in marriage.

FIFTEEN

Over breakfast on Friday morning, Anna sat down at the table with Joel. They had a few minutes before Joel needed to go back out and continue the day's work.

He looked curiously at Anna, as she never sat during breakfast. Something was up.

Anna took a small ring box out of her apron pocket and handed it to Joel.

"Here is the ring your father gave me," she said. "If you would like to give it to Belle as an engagement ring, you may."

It was a beautiful gold ring set with a mine-cut diamond in the center between two small cushion-shaped rubies. Joel knew Belle would love the ring.

"When he gave it to me, your father told me that the rubies symbolize love and that the diamond symbolizes eternity. I know he would have loved for you to give it to your bride," she said softly.

"But I hate to take it from you. I know it meant so much to you and that he saved for so long to buy it for you. Are you sure?" he asked.

"I am sure. Nothing would give me more pleasure than to see it on Belle's hand. It would feel like your father is a part of our lives still," she smiled sadly. "I still miss him almost every day."

"I know you do. I wish so much that he were here, too. But if Bill sees it, won't he be upset? I thought he suggested that you sell it a while back."

"No, in the end I did not want to sell it, and he was fine with that. This was his idea, for you to have the ring," she said. "He does care about you,

Joel, more than you know."

"Maybe I will go in and talk to him about the conversation I aim to have with Mr. Westlake on Sunday to ask for Belle's hand. Perhaps he can give me some advice," Joel said thoughtfully.

"I am sure that would mean a lot to him," she replied. "There is so little that makes him happy these days."

Joel talked with Bill the next morning. After offering some advice, Bill said to him, "Son, I did not do right by you. I hope you can forgive me."

In that moment, Joel felt a weight lifted from his heart. He was able to forgive him. "Of course, Bill. I appreciate all you did for Ma and for me."

Bill smiled and immediately drifted off, as he was inclined to do these days. It was obvious that he did not have much time left.

On Sunday morning, Joel got up before the sunrise and rushed through his chores as quickly as he could. His farmhand came out early to help.

Joel hurried inside when he was done, washed his face, put on his old Sunday best clothing and wolfed down a quick breakfast. He jumped on his horse and headed to town.

By the time he arrived, church was almost out so he waited for Mr. Westlake on the Hughes' front porch. He was so nervous that his hands were shaking. He tried taking deep breaths to calm himself down.

Soon, William Westlake rode up to the house. Joel hurried down the steps to help Belle and her mother out of the buggy. After greeting the ladies, he turned to face Belle's stepfather.

"Sir, I am wondering if I could speak to you for a few minutes?" he asked politely.

"All right," William said curtly.

Belle and her mother hurried by them, and the men sat on the porch.

Joel cleared his throat. "Sir, as you know, I have been courting Belle for over a year now. She means everything to me. I am set to inherit my father's farm very soon. I believe I can make a good living."

William looked at him with no expression.

Here goes nothing, Joel thought.

"With that in mind, I would like to ask your daughter to marry me and am humbly asking for your blessing. Although we are young, I am confident we are ready to be married."

William continued to look at Joel in silence. At last, he asked, "Does Belle know you are speaking to me about this?"

"Yes sir, I believe she does."

"Why don't we get through the summer, then see where you are on the farm financially? Depending on the weather, it could be a great year for winter hay, or another terrible one. The almanac predicts another drought," William said.

"I hope not. But even if it is another bad summer, we will figure it out. It is hard for Belle and me to see each other, as I cannot really leave the farm for any length of time. That is why we would like to be wed sooner rather than later."

"Well, of course after September when Belle turns twenty-one, we cannot stop you from marrying if you are both bound and determined to do so. So, if you want to become engaged now, that is fine. I give my permission. But her mother and I request that you wait until after the summer for the wedding to see where you are on the farm. Plus, she will want to give Belle a big church wedding, and that takes time to plan."

"Oh, thank you, sir!" Joel said. "May I speak to Belle, now?"

"Of course. However, we will need to leave in a few minutes for home. And good luck on the farm. We will all need it this summer." William left the porch to call Belle.

When Belle came out to the porch, she looked nervous. "Is everything all right?"

"Why don't we walk to the park?" Joel suggested. "I know you have to leave soon, but I just want a few minutes with you before you go."

"That is fine. I am already packed," she answered, smiling at him.

The couple walked slowly; hands clasped. It was a beautiful spring morning. When they reached the park, which was surprisingly empty for a Sunday morning, they made their way to the gazebo. There, Joel knelt in front of Belle.

"Belle, would you do me the honor of becoming my wife?" he asked in a shaky voice.

Belle's eyes filled with tears. "Oh yes!"

She looked surprised when Joel took a ring box from his pocket. He opened the box, and showed her the ring.

"It is beautiful!" she whispered. "But Joel, how did you ever afford this?"

"It was the ring my father gave my mother when they were engaged," he said, standing up. "Let's see if it fits."

The ring fit perfectly.

Belle looked up at Joel, eyes shining. "I will treasure it always. It is perfect! Oh, Joel!" She threw herself into his arms.

Joel looked around and seeing no one close by, leaned down and kissed her.

The couple walked back to the Hughes house slowly, admiring the ring on Belle's finger. They went into the house to share their happy news.

SIXTEEN

Belle

- *October 1889* -

Belle got up early on the crisp fall morning. It was here—her wedding day. She was marrying Joel today.

The past few months had been difficult for Belle and Joel. First of all, they rarely saw each other—it was just too far. Secondly, the drought did return, and Joel—and Belle's stepfather—lost quite a few head of cattle, as did all the ranchers in the Midwest. Finally, Bill suffered in agony throughout the summer drought and died in September, never seeing his son Billy again.

Belle's mother had designed her wedding to be one of the highlights of the season. Belle protested that it was too much– that Joel and she didn't need all that– but her mother insisted.

She had hoped that Missy and Billy could come to their wedding, but Missy just wasn't up to it with a newborn, plus they certainly had no money for the train fare. Their daughter Esmerelda—Ezzie for short-- had been born in mid-August and was named for Billy's mother. The new parents were thrilled with their baby girl, but life was hard on their claim. They struggled to make ends meet, so much so that Billy couldn't even come home to say goodbye to his father.

Of course, Belle had her ten-year-old sister Beatrice for a flower girl, but she had really wanted Missy as her matron of honor. Instead, she asked an old school friend to step in.

Amos, who was to be Joel's best man, traveled with his family to Cameron the day before and stayed at a boarding house in the town. Joel's mother arrived that evening with Joel's Uncle Don, and the three of them stayed at a hotel in Cameron.

The couple would marry at the Presbyterian Church in Cameron followed by a noon wedding breakfast. After that, they would spend their first night together at the finest hotel in Cameron. That was a wedding gift from Joel's Uncle Don.

"You should not have to spend your wedding night covered in dust after an eight-hour trip home," he told Joel after he had made the arrangements.

His mother's gift to him was a beautiful new dark blue morning coat with white shirt, white waistcoat, and lavender trousers. His future father-in-law had gifted him a white bowtie. The Frasers had purchased top hats for both Amos and Joel and he shined up his best boots for the occasion. Joel barely recognized himself in all the finery. He hoped so much that Belle would be pleased.

Belle was thrilled that they were to spend their first night as a married couple at the Hotel Cameron. It was a swanky place with gorgeous red carpets and crystal chandeliers. The couple would spend their wedding afternoon after the reception walking around town and enjoying the day. Joel had made reservations for dinner at the hotel, which was said to have the finest cuisine in Cameron. Then, there would be the wedding night.

As much as she desired to be with Joel, Belle did not know what to think about that. Her mother had told her some of the basics, but it all sounded so confusing, frankly a little embarrassing, and possibly uncomfortable. Would she have to bare her body in front of Joel? What would he do? She blushed, just thinking about it. Her mother had said that some women really liked the "marriage act," but Belle was not so sure.

I hope I can please him, she thought. Her mother had said that was important. But as she did not know what she was doing, how would that be possible?

I won't think about that now, she decided. *I'll worry about that tonight.*

Belle jumped out of bed and examined her gorgeous white wedding dress again. Her mother had sent for it from New York and it had arrived the week before. It was silk brocade with a fitted waist and a train. Small white embroidered flowers decorated the bodice. Of course, it had fashionable leg-o-mutton sleeves, one of her favorite looks. Her long lace veil would cover her face until Joel lifted it for their first kiss as a married couple. Belle had white kid gloves that would tuck under the sleeves with a slit on one finger so Joel could slip the ring on her finger. Her mother had surprised her with white satin slippers with a one-inch heel. It was all so beautiful. She couldn't wait until Joel saw her walking down the aisle in all her finery.

"Here we are!" cried her mother and younger sister as they entered the room. "It's time to start getting ready."

"Then you can put on your wedding dress," Beatrice piped in with shining eyes. "I can't wait to put my pretty new dress on too!"

"I just hope you're not prettier than the bride," teased Belle. "Maybe Joel will want to marry you instead!"

"Oh no, I hope not," Beatrice gasped with big round eyes. "Do I have to?"

Belle and her mother laughed. "I'm just teasing you," Belle said. "Why don't you come help wash my hair?" They made their way down to the washroom, where the tub was ready with steaming hot water.

After her hair was washed, her sister left the room. Belle finished her bath alone, scrubbing herself thoroughly. She climbed out of the deep tub and was drying herself off, looking down at her body. Would Joel think she was desirable? What would he look like with no clothes? She blushed and quickly made her way back to the bedroom, wrapped in the large towel.

Her mother and Beatrice helped her dress in a new chemise, drawers, and stockings. She even had a new corset, which she grumbled was not as comfortable as her old one.

"You cannot wear that old thing to your wedding," her mother had said when she asked to wear her old one instead. "It barely cinches your waist!"

Since the dress was fitted, she only wore one petticoat. Beatrice helped her to attach the supports for the leg-o-mutton sleeves. Finally, they carefully pulled the dress over her head, trying not to ruin her beautiful Gibson-girl bouffant hairstyle that her mother's maid had styled for her after her bath. Her mother carefully attached the veil to the top of her bouffant. Beatrice helped her put on the wedding shoes as Belle could hardly bend down in the new corset. When all was finished, she pulled on the special white wedding gloves and then finally took a look at herself in her mother's looking glass. She gasped at the beautiful bride looking back.

Her mother's eyes filled with tears and Beatrice sighed. Belle just stared in wonder.

An hour later, Belle walked down the aisle on her stepfather's arm, her heart full of happiness. As she approached Joel, she felt as if she was in a dream. Joel was so handsome in his wedding clothes. He looked at her with such intensity and love.

It had been a tough summer apart, especially with the drought and worry about the cattle dying. But here they were, ready to start their life together. It would be hard at first with all the challenges on the farm, but she trusted they would weather it together.

Before she knew it, their vows were said and Joel was kissing her. The ceremony was over, she was now Joel's wife. What a strange but joyous feeling those words brought up in her. Finally, they could be together every day and every night.

The couple walked back down the aisle looking neither left nor right, as was the custom. They stood to the side with their parents while people piled out of the church to form an aisle of two lines with William's fine carriage at the end. Beatrice had decorated the carriage with crepe and flowers that morning so Joel and Belle could leave the church in style. Belle and Joel ran down the aisle while the guests threw rice at them for luck. Joel helped her into the carriage, jumped in, and they headed to her parents' house for their wedding breakfast.

The wedding breakfast consisted of delicious pastries, tea, coffee, chocolates, and their wedding cake. It was three-tiered with white fondant and a beautiful cake topper of a bride and groom. There were several tables covered in white cloths and flowers, set with her mother's finest china place settings and silver. It was an elegant but small affair, with only close friends and relatives in attendance. Belle enjoyed the breakfast but was glad when it was over. She had never been comfortable being the center of attention.

Joel and Belle left the breakfast waving goodbye to their guests as they drove off in Joel's buggy. Once out of sight, Joel pulled the buggy over and kissed his wife passionately.

"I cannot wait until tonight," he whispered, looking in her eyes.

At that moment, Belle quit worrying about the night ahead. This was Joel. Being with him could not be anything but wonderful. It was all she wanted.

Joel and Belle made their way to the studio in town for a wedding photograph. Next, they would return to the hotel, change clothes, and walk around the town.

"I will meet you at the hotel after your photograph to help you change for the last time," her mother had told her. "From then on, you will have your husband to help you."

Joel and Belle had a delightful day, strolling around the little town of Cameron and driving to the nearby Lake Burlington to watch the sunset.

"It's the first sunset of our married life," Joel said to Belle. "Shall we go back to the hotel for dinner?"

"Yes, please. And then I'm off to bed—I am tired!" She blushed crimson as she realized what she had just said.

"I agree, it's been a very exciting day," he said gently. "I am a bit tired myself."

He then grinned at her and said, "But not too tired."

Belle looked at Joel for a second, shocked, and then she laughed. "You scamp!"

Dinner looked delicious, but Belle could hardly eat a bite, she was so nervous. What if she was no good at the physical side of marriage? She tried not to worry, but she did not really know what she was supposed to do. What if she let Joel down? Would she be a good wife to him in that way?

Too soon for Belle, they finished their meal and headed up to their room.

The room had beautiful red and gold wallpaper with golden sconces and a thick red rug. There was a large mahogany four poster bed, a gold brocade settee, a table and chairs, a chest for clothing, and even a place where one could hang clothes on hooks in something called a closet. Attached was a dressing room and an indoor privy with a tub. Belle had marveled at the room earlier when her mother helped her change from her wedding dress, but now she was too nervous to appreciate its many charms.

Once in the room she turned to him. "I don't know what you expect of me," she said, blushing. "I don't want you to be disappointed."

"Oh, Belle," Joel said tenderly. "You could never disappoint me. We are both new to this. I think the idea for tonight is for us to explore each other. Why don't I help you unbutton your dress, and then you can put your nightgown on if you feel comfortable with that."

He paused for a moment. "My Uncle Don had some wine sent up. Perhaps we can have a glass of that after you change?"

Belle's eyes grew large. "I have never had wine before. Do you think it is all right?"

"Yes, Mrs. Watson. You are a married woman now. Now turn around and I will unbutton you. You get comfortable in your nightgown, and then we can taste the wine," he smiled.

Belle made her way to the dressing room. Joel went over to the window and opened it a little. He could hear someone playing the fiddle below.

In a few minutes, Belle walked out in her white lawn nightgown. Joel gulped. He could see right through the thin gown to her beautiful body. Trying to restrain himself, he looked away and poured them both a small glass of wine. They sat together on the settee, sipping their wine.

After they finished their glasses, Joel was not sure what to do next. But as luck would have it, the fiddle player below began to play a tune they had danced to many times before. It happened to be a particular favorite of Belle's—"Adieu False Heart."

Joel stood up and bowed. "May I have this dance, Mrs. Watson?" he asked formally.

As they swayed to the music, Joel began to kiss Belle gently, first on the neck, and then he moved the gown off her shoulder and kissed it. He kissed her mouth, then stepped back and removed his shirt and trousers. He then pulled the top of her gown down some more and began kissing the top of her breasts. Soon, Belle began to breathe more quickly. She was starting to feel that desire grow hot inside of her. She wanted Joel.

As he pushed the gown off of her body, he could see that she was naked underneath. He gently walked her to the bed where they laid down facing each other, kissing with more and more passion.

After some time, he moved his hand down her body. As he began to gently caress her, Belle's eyes opened in surprise. She had never felt such a sensation before.

Time seemed to stand still. Belle was beginning to pant and arched her back. It was all Joel could do to stay slow and gentle. He whispered to Belle what he was going to do next. Joel eased his finger inside her. As he began to move his finger slowly he used his thumb to gently caress her.

"Oh, I like that," she groaned.

After a while, Joel climbed on top of her and slowly guided himself into her. Belle could feel Joel's erection inside her. She thrust her hips toward him and groaned as he pushed inside her.

"Ouch!" she cried.

"Should I stop?" he asked anxiously.

"No, no, it's alright," she said. "Just go slowly."

Joel slowed down and moved gently while kissing her breasts. All of a sudden, he groaned and thrust deep inside her, crying out in ecstasy.

When he recovered, he rolled off her and kissed her tenderly. "Are you alright?" he whispered. "I know it hurt you."

"Oh yes, I am fine," Belle assured him, cheeks flushed. "It hurt a little bit but I was prepared for that from my mother. She promised me it would not be as uncomfortable next time and then stop hurting completely after a while. But she never told me it would feel like this."

Belle paused. "Did I do it right?" she asked in a small voice.

"Oh, yes, my darling wife. I promise I will find ways to pleasure you more next time. I would try now, but it seems like you are a bit sore."

"Yes. But when can the next time be?" Belle asked. "Can we do this every night?"

"Well, I don't know," Joel answered slowly. "I imagine we can do it as much as we like."

"Can we do it again tomorrow?" she asked. "I probably won't be so sore then."

"Certainly, my love," Joel kissed her deeply. "But now let's clean up and then get some sleep. We have a lot to do tomorrow—ride back to our home, unpack your things, not to mention make love again."

"Is that what you call it?" Belle asked. "I think I am going to really like making love."

"I think I am too."

The next morning Joel woke up before the sun, disoriented at first. Then he turned over and saw his beautiful bride. She was sound asleep with a sweet innocent look on her face.

He started to get hard, just looking at her. She opened her eyes and looked at him—first with surprise, then with joy.

"Good morning, my dear," Joel said in a husky voice. "How are you feeling this morning?"

Belle leaned over to kiss him and discovered his erection. "Can we do it again?" she whispered.

Joel groaned. "Of course, but aren't you a bit tender down there? We could wait another day or so."

"Oh no, I wouldn't want to wait! And I'm not sore, not really. Can I touch it?"

"If you do, this will be a very short lovemaking session," he grinned. "Let me touch you first."

Joel took his time, caressing her slowly, gently. She began breathing faster and faster, then moaning until she finally cried out. Joel then gently pushed inside her and they rocked together, kissing and moaning. His climax was so intense it shook them both.

After they finished Belle asked in wonder, "Is this what it is always like?"

"I don't know, Belle. I guess we will have to find out."

"Tonight?" she asked shyly.

Joel smiled. "Tonight, and every night you wish. But right now, I think we need to get going. It is an eight-hour buggy ride, and the sun is beginning to rise."

"Can't we just stay for a while longer?" she asked, snuggling closer to him. "I like being in bed with you."

"I like it too, and I wish we could stay in here all day, but we must go. The sooner we arrive home, the sooner we can make love again."

"Oh, all right," she grumbled. She got out of bed, stretched her naked body. Joel could hardly restrain himself from pulling her back. Instead, he got up quickly and splashed cold water from the washbasin on his face.

The couple left the hotel an hour later after a quick breakfast in the hotel restaurant of eggs, bacon, and coffee. While Belle purchased some food for their noontime meal that would be on the road, Joel grabbed Blue at the stable and hitched him to the buggy.

Belle put her hand on Joel's knee as they started out.

"I'm going to put us into a ditch if you don't stop distracting me." he grinned. "Better keep your hands to yourself, Mrs. Watson!"

Belle sighed and moved her hand away. They rode on, stopping only once during the morning to stretch their legs. As they walked around hand in hand, it took every bit of willpower Joel had to keep from laying Belle down on the tall grass and making love to her right there. To his delight, after they stopped for their noontime meal, Belle grabbed the picnic blanket, took Joel's hand and walked him over to a big maple tree. There, in the shade of the tree, out in the middle of the Missouri prairie, the couple made love again.

Afterwards, they lay in each other's arms, feeling the soft breeze—spent and so happy.

'I think I am going to love being married," Belle sighed.

"I know I am going to love being married to you," Joel said softly, kissed her, and helped her to her feet. It was time to go home.

A few hours later, they rode up just as the sun was about to set.

"We're home!" Joel said cheerfully. The couple smiled at each other, climbed out of the buggy, and began their lives together.

SEVENTEEN

Joel

- October, 1890 -

Joel rode back toward the house from his cattle pasture. He was bone tired. His milk cow Sadie had calved in the middle of the night, and then another couple of cattle had gotten sick with what he feared might be Texas cattle fever. He knew he should send for the vet, but they just couldn't afford it. He already owed him too much. But if the sick cattle didn't improve soon, he would have to send for him, debt or no debt.

They were down to only twenty-five head, from thirty-five the year before. They still had their milk cow Sadie; the calf Bessie had birthed a few years before. Bessie had died, which was a blessing as they didn't have the money to feed her anyway. Belle and his mother watched over the chickens and had a nice-sized chicken coop. They still owned three pigs, but he was going to have to sell one to buy more winter wheat and pay off the vet.

On top of all that, his horse Blue was beginning to show her age, and Bill's old horse had died last summer.

I might need a new horse soon, he thought bleakly. He still had the one farmhand, but with his financial situation, Joel was not sure he could keep him on.

As he neared the house, he perked up. It was their one-year wedding anniversary, and Belle had told him she would cook a special dinner. His mother had smiled and said she would take a tray in her room that night, to give them privacy.

Belle had also mentioned that she had a surprise for their anniversary. When he heard that, he knew he had to find something special for Belle as well, so he conferred with his mother.

"She was admiring a beautiful set of combs with jeweled designs in the general store last week," his mother informed him. But they were dear—$1.52.

He just had $3.00 left from the calf they'd sold last spring. As much as he hated to deplete the last of their cash, he decided to dip into that money to get Belle the combs. What could be more important than seeing his wife smile?

When Joel went in the store to buy them, kindly Mr. Osbourne said he would give the combs to him with the "first anniversary discount" and sold them to him for $1.32. Joel doubted there existed such a discount, but was happy to receive it anyway.

He stopped in the mudroom to remove his jacket, boots and hat. Whistling, he came into the kitchen and went over to kiss Belle's cheek. "Mmm, that smells good!" he exclaimed. "What are we having?"

"Go change out of your dirty clothes and I will tell you when you return," she replied with a smile.

"Did Ma go upstairs already?"

"Yes, and I fed your helper George on the porch. He went back to the bunkhouse already. So, it is just you and me tonight," she said.

Nuzzling her neck, Joel said gruffly, "Can you help me change? I'm pretty tired…"

"You aren't fooling me, sir. You will just have to wait for that until after dinner. Now hurry and go get changed," she said and pushed him toward the stairs.

Joel quickly washed himself and put on his Sunday best. He combed his hair and grabbed Belle's gift, which his mother had wrapped in a piece of brightly colored cotton fabric. He decided to give it to her after dinner.

As he came back into the kitchen, Belle was dishing out a fragrant chicken stew into two bowls, along with biscuits and a bottle of ale. On the sideboard, Joel could see a pie.

"Is that an apple pie?" he asked, sniffing the air. "It's my favorite pie!"

"I can't take credit for that," she replied. "That was your mother. She made it for our anniversary."

"This entire meal is all my favorites," Joel said happily. "Thanks for such a wonderful surprise."

"Oh, no, this isn't your surprise," Belle said, smirking. "You'll have to wait a bit longer for that."

"Well, give me a hint. Do we need to be in the bedroom for my surprise?" he asked.

"Joel! You are so bad," she said, blushing. "No, we don't have to be, but perhaps it is a good idea."

Joel took her hand. "I'm just teasing you. But I will say our bedroom is my favorite room in the house."

Belle giggled as they began to eat the delicious dinner. Joel looked at Belle thoughtfully as they ate. She looked tired—laundry, cooking, cleaning, sewing, taking care of the chickens, milking the cow—even with Anna's help she worked hard all day long. He had noticed that the last few months all the constant work was starting to take a toll on her. She seemed more tired than usual.

But she never complained. Sometimes, he just couldn't believe she was his. Sure, times were tough but they were so happy together.

"Why are you looking at me like that?" Belle asked.

"Just realizing what a treasure I have in you," he said, taking her hand.

"I feel the same way," she said, squeezing his hand.

After finishing off a second piece of pie, Joel offered to help with the dishes.

"No, no," Belle insisted. "Go sit down in the parlor and rest. I'll be as quick as I can."

"Please hurry," Joel begged. "I don't think I can wait much longer."

But washing dishes was not a quick and easy task. It required two pans, one for washing the dishes, the other for scalding. Belle was lucky to have a good-sized wooden sink—Joel's father had put that in when he plumbed in the hand pump years ago—so she placed the washing pan with her homemade lye soap in the sink. She pumped in cold water, added in some hot water from the teakettle and shook the cake of soap to make suds. After the dishes were washed, Belle stacked them into a big pan that she had placed on the table. She then poured the rest of the hot water from the teakettle over the dishes to scald them. She swept the floor and wiped off the table while they cooled off and finally dried them and put the dishes away.

By the time Belle finished the dishes and made her way to the parlor, Joel was fast asleep. Poor man—he was exhausted. She sat in the rocking chair near him and let him sleep, while knitting a little blanket.

About twenty minutes later, Joel startled awake and looked ruefully at Belle. "I'm so sorry I fell asleep," he said, kneeling in front of her. "But I am awake now. Shall I give you your anniversary gift?"

"Oh Joel, I hope you didn't spend any money. Just being married to you is gift enough."

"No, it isn't! And I wanted to get you something special. We will never have another one-year anniversary again. I am so grateful for our life together."

"Oh, sweetheart," she said, eyes welling. "I am so grateful for you."

Joel handed her the fabric-wrapped gift.

Belle opened it and gasped. "Joel! I saw these in the store and loved them. But they are so dear—can we afford them?"

"Mr. Osbourne gave me a first-anniversary discount, so they didn't bankrupt us. Try them on."

"Let's go upstairs, and I will try them on up there, " she said. "I want to give you your gift up there."

They extinguished the oil lamps and lit a candle to take upstairs. Joel closed the door to their bedroom and placed the candle on the bureau. Belle closed the curtains and asked Joel to unbutton her and loosen her stays, but then sit back and close his eyes.

"I can't wait too long," he groaned.

"I'll be quick," she promised. Belle took off her clothes, and then put the combs in her hair.

"You can open your eyes now. How do the combs look?" she asked.

Her beautiful body was luminescent in the candlelight.

"Oh Belle," he said softly. "You are so beautiful."

Belle walked over to him and took his hand, placing it on her belly. "Your gift will be here in four months," she told him, eyes shining.

Joel buried his head in her belly. "What? You mean a baby? Oh, my love. I'm so happy!"

He quickly removed his clothes and pulled her to him. After kissing her deeply he asked, "Is it safe for us to make love? I don't want to hurt our baby."

"Yes," she assured him. "I asked the midwife when I saw her in town. She looked a bit shocked, but told me it is fine until I go into labor."

Groaning, he said, "I want to be inside you." He pulled her down, and thrust himself inside.

"Oh yes, oh Joel," she moaned. He thrust himself over and over until he cried out.

After he rolled off her, he began to caress her, kiss her belly, then moved his mouth down. Belle moaned louder and louder.

"Sssh," Joel laughed. "You'll wake up Ma!" But he continued to use his tongue to make her writhe and finally gasp in pleasure.

"Oh Joel," she said afterward. "I hope we can always stay this close together. I love you so much."

"I love you too, my darling. We will be like this forever. I will make sure of it. Soon we will have our baby, the child we have been dreaming of."

They fell asleep in each other's arms, exhausted but happy.

EIGHTEEN

Belle

- Christmas 1890 -

Christmas morning was a cold one. Belle woke up slowly, hearing some noises coming from the kitchen. Of course, Joel was long gone doing chores so that he could eat an early breakfast with them.

They had a houseful of visitors. Belle's parents, her sister Beatrice, and the Westlake's housekeeper Mrs. Ware had traveled to Belle's new home that day. Mary Westlake decided to bring Mrs. Ware as a way of easing the burden of so many visitors on Belle, who was now seven months pregnant.

Belle slipped out of bed, used the chamber pot and washed herself quickly with the freezing water from her pitcher and basin. She attempted to put on the maternity corset that her mother had brought her from Cameron, but had to call on Beatrice for help. She had let out two dresses for her pregnancy, and Beatrice helped her put on the nicest one.

Once she was dressed, Belle shooed Beatrice off to get dressed and then made her way downstairs. She wanted to help with the Christmas breakfast. She walked carefully down the stairs as she was getting more and more unwieldy. Only seven more weeks to go, she hoped. Of course, it could be sooner than that. The midwife had guessed sometime mid-to-late February. Belle hoped it would be sooner rather than later.

Missy had written to her about Ezzie's birth. She described how the pains started and how she got through the hard labor—by biting on a stick and screaming so loudly that she scared Billy. She did not sugar-coat it.

"You must be prepared for it to hurt more than anything you've ever felt before. It is not easy, but so worth it. Make sure you have a good mid-wife like I did. I suppose it wasn't that bad because I am in the family way again," she had written.

Belle dreaded that part. Would she be able to stand the pain without screaming out too much? Would the baby be healthy? Would she survive the birth herself? Just last summer a friend of Joel's from school died two days after giving birth to a healthy baby. One of the ladies in town told her that she just "got a fever and then bled and bled. Dr. Walter couldn't stop it, so she died."

But today was Christmas, so she must not dwell on such negative thoughts. She had their two families together. They were to have an early breakfast, take the two families' enclosed buggies to church and then back home. There had been no snow yet—which was unusual for December—so the roads were clear.

There were quite a few gifts under the Christmas tree in the parlor. Her stepfather and sister had helped to put it up and decorate it the night before. They put a few candles on some branches and lit them, but blew them out quickly when Joel got nervous about the fire hazard.

As she entered the kitchen, she could see her mother and Mrs. Ware preparing the Christmas tom turkey Joel had shot yesterday. Anna was busy making flapjacks and frying bacon.

"Happy Christmas!" Belle said while entering the kitchen. "What should I do to help?"

"Perhaps you could make the coffee?" Anna answered. "Joel should be in soon with the eggs, although we won't have many in this cold."

"I'll make the coffee and then help him find the eggs," Belle replied. "I know where the hens lay them in the barn."

The Frasers had given them a coffee percolator for a wedding gift the year before. The percolator worked using steam pressure by boiling the water inside. When the water boiled, steam pressure was created and the water rose over the coffee grounds, which in turn made delicious coffee. It was a marvel.

Just then, they heard a loud clatter on the stairs. It was Beatrice, of course.

"May I go look and see what Santa brought me?" she asked.

"Yes, you may," her mother answered, and dried her hands to walk into the parlor with Beatrice. William was already in the parlor, waiting.

From the kitchen, Belle could hear Beatrice squeal with excitement. "It's a doll bed! With blankets and sheets—and even a pillow—and a nightgown! Flora is going to love it!"

Flora was the doll that Santa had brought her on the previous Christmas. She took Flora everywhere—she was her constant companion.

Her Pa had made the doll bed out of the walnut from one of the trees that had fallen on his farm. He could only work on it at night, when Beatrice was fast asleep.

Her mother had made the bedding, pillow, a little mattress, and Flora's nightgown. She also made a matching nightgown for Beatrice, which was wrapped up and under the tree.

Next, Beatrice got into her stocking, which contained an orange, some chocolate coins, a peppermint stick, and a silver dollar. At the very bottom of the stocking was a little gold ring with a tiny garnet. Beatrice oohed and awed over the ring and then put it on.

"It fits perfectly. How did Santa know?" Beatrice asked excitedly.

"Actually, your pa put that in there," Belle heard her mother answer. Belle remembered William giving her a little ring when she was Beatrice's age. It was a bit small now, but sometimes she wore it on her pinky.

Belle smiled to herself as she listened to Beatrice's exclamations of joy. Someday soon she would have a child of her own squealing over Christmas. She couldn't wait.

After she put the percolator on the stove, Belle threw on an old coat of Joel's, the only one that fit her now. She walked out in the crisp cold morning. The farm had a thin layer of frost—that must have happened last night—and the sparkling white landscape was breathtaking. Looking around for Joel, she found him in the barn pitching hay down from the loft.

"Merry Christmas!" she called out.

"Merry Christmas! I'll be down in a minute."

Belle walked to the chicken coop at the back of the barn. She was proud of her twelve hens and her bandy rooster. Their two dogs, Rex and Pal, kept the chickens safe from foxes and coyotes, but during the winter the chickens laid fewer eggs as it was too cold. Joel had the idea to build a chicken coop in the barn for the winter months. The hens were not fond of cold weather, but the coop in the barn helped to keep them laying.

Belle fed the chickens some scraps from the previous night's dinner and then went to gather their eggs. Most of the eggs were in the coop, but for some reason, a couple of their hens like to lay their eggs on the shelves under the loft. There were only eight eggs today, but that would have to do.

Joel climbed down just as she was finishing. "Where's my Christmas kiss?" he asked, smiling at his beautiful wife, whose cheeks were glowing from the cold.

Joel pulled Belle to him, kissing her passionately. She responded in kind. Joel was constantly surprised by the passion his wife showed him, especially since she was pregnant. They kissed again.

"Shall we go upstairs, my love?" he whispered.

"I wish!" she replied, and he kissed her again.

"Whoa! Looks like chores are not getting done," called a voice from across the barn. William walked toward them, grinning. "Your mother sent me out here to check on where the eggs were. But I see you are busy."

"I'm coming!" Belle answered, blushing again. She hurried past her stepfather back to the house.

"Ah, to be young again and newly married," William sighed. "Enjoy it while you can. Once the baby comes, her attention will be diverted."

Joel looked down. "Perhaps," he murmured. But he really did not think so. He believed they had something that would never change. Their intense love and passion for each other was all-consuming.

As the family sat down to Christmas breakfast, Belle looked around the table. How fortunate she was! Despite the financial difficulties on the farm—which frankly, were pretty concerning—she had never been happier. And here she sat with their two families on Christmas day, a new baby on the way. How lucky could one girl get?

But then a different thought popped into her head, "*This is the last happy day you will have.*" She shook her head trying to rid herself of that bad feeling. Where was that coming from?

Belle asked to lead the prayer before the meal. As they joined hands, Belle prayed: "Thank you, God, for sending your only son to us so that we may be saved. Lord, thank you for each member of this family, for this bounty, and for all our worldly goods. Keep us safe and help us in these hard times. We thank you for our new baby and ask that you keep him or her healthy and safe. Amen."

The prayer made her feel marginally better.

"Amen!" shouted Beatrice. "Can we eat now?"

The meal was a merry one. Beatrice chattered excitedly about her gifts from Santa, and wondered aloud what gifts Belle had under the tree for her. Each member of the family—and Mrs. Ware—predicted as to whether the baby would be a boy or a girl. They all guessed a boy—except Beatrice who wanted a baby girl playmate.

Belle kept up the pretense of happiness, but a nagging feeling that something bad was going to happen wouldn't leave her. It felt like a black cloud was hanging over her head.

But she didn't say anything. *Why ruin Christmas for everyone?* she thought.

When the meal was over, they quickly bundled up for the cold ride to church. Mrs. Ware said it was too cold and she would stay home and do the dishes.

"Can I ride with Belle?" asked Beatrice.

"If it is all right with Joel and Belle," William answered.

"Of course," Belle replied. "We need more sister time."

The parents piled into William's carriage while Belle, Joel, and Beatrice crammed into Joel's enclosed buggy.

"We will need to hurry along if we are to arrive on time," William shouted to Joel. He urged his horses and off they went at a fast clip.

"Hmmm. Well, I am not driving too fast with you two ladies in here," Joel said to Belle. "Do you care if we are late?"

"No, it's fine," answered Belle.

"I don't care if we miss the whole service!" Beatrice giggled. "Let's go extra slow!"

"Now, Beatrice. Joel, let's not go too slow," Belle said. "I don't want to upset Mother."

"Of course," Joel answered. "Now Beatrice, tell me about your teacher. I understand she is very strict?"

As Beatrice chattered away, Joel kept an eye on the sky. A few minutes later, dark clouds had rolled in and were looking menacing.

"Looks like we might finally get some snow. I wonder if we should turn back?" he asked Belle. "I wouldn't want to get caught in a bad storm."

"But our mothers will surely worry if we don't show up," Belle replied.

"I am hoping they will come back as well," Joel answered. Making the decision, he turned the buggy around.

By the time they arrived back at the farm, the wind had picked up and snow was falling fast. The girls went inside as Joel unhitched the buggy and took care of Blue.

After just a few minutes snow shower became a squall and the wind began to scream and howl.

"This is turning into a blizzard," Joel said. "Hopefully our folks are at church and will stay there until it passes." He went outside to tie a rope from the front porch to the barn door, in case the snowstorm became too blinding to see.

"I'm sure they are staying at church," Belle said confidently, mindful of Beatrice's many worried looks outside. But again, she had a sinking feeling—something was not right.

NINETEEN

Anna

Anna, William, and Mary went at a fast clip toward town, hoping to make it to church before services began. William kept looking out of the buggy at the sky. As they passed the Hadley's farm, the wind picked up and snow began to fall.

"Should we turn around?" Mary asked William.

"No, I think this will blow through pretty quickly," he said. "We are thirty minutes away from town. We might have to stay at your sister-in-law's house for a while, though, at least until it stops snowing."

"I hope that our children get there safely," Anna said.

"Joel is pretty sensible," William offered. "I am sure they will turn around if he is worried. They are quite a ways behind us, as Joel doesn't have a two-horse carriage like ours."

Within ten minutes, the weather had gone from bad to worse. William could not see the road anymore. But he knew if he stopped, they would be doomed.

He continued to go slowly, hoping that he was still on the road. The women were quiet —they could see nothing but a blinding white vista. A coyote ran out in front of the horses, spooking them. The predator, along with the storm, caused the horses to panic. They bolted, went down into a ditch and the carriage turned over.

When Anna came to, she was lying on the ceiling of the carriage. She could not see William or Mary. The snow had become a blizzard. She was bleeding from the head, which hurt quite badly—but knew she must get out and find the Westlakes. They needed shelter or they would all perish.

When she crawled out of the carriage, she saw one of the horses, lying in the ditch making a terrible sound. Its leg was broken, poor thing. Anna knew the right thing to do was to kill it, but she had no gun. The other horse seemed to have disappeared.

Anna finally stood up and called out for the Westlakes. She could neither see nor hear them. She began to drag her skirts, walking back toward the Hadleys' farm. Or so she thought.

It was the wrong direction.

Anna walked and walked through the blizzard, until she could walk no more. Her head was pounding fiercely. She knew if she didn't find shelter soon, she would freeze to death.

But there was no shelter to be found. She finally sat down and cried until she was numb enough to fall asleep.

. . .

Back on the farm as the day wore on, the blizzard did not let up. Instead, it intensified. Joel went out from time to time to take care of the animals. Belle and Beatrice stayed inside, taking turns reading aloud from the bible. After a while, they could smell the turkey that Mrs. Ware had put in the oven when they had arrived back home. Mrs. Ware, Belle, and Beatrice went ahead and made the Christmas dinner that their mother had started cooking that morning.

The blizzard continued. At 3:00, the three of them, along with Mrs. Ware, sat down to dinner as they were famished. Belle and Joel tried to distract Beatrice with funny stories about their school years. Beatrice also had a lot of questions about their courtship.

"Why did you decide to get married?" she asked. "Is it because you wanted a baby? I know you can't have one unless you're married. That's what Ma told me."

Joel looked at Belle. Mrs. Ware snorted.

"Well, yes, of course we wanted a baby," Belle answered. "And you are not supposed to have a baby if you aren't married. But that is not why we got married."

"Why did you, then?" Beatrice asked.

Joel took Belle's hand from across the table. "Because we fell in love," he said, kissing Belle's hand.

Belle blushed. "Yes, that is why," she said shyly. 'I hope you will marry for love someday too, Beatrice."

"I will," Beatrice sighed. "It is so romantic."

Belle brought out the Christmas plum pudding. "Let's save some for Ma, Pa, and Miss Anna," she said to Beatrice. "So take just a small amount."

After they finished, Belle and Mrs. Ware did the dishes while Beatrice swept the floor.

Joel went out to check on the livestock. The blizzard had died down some, but he still had to use the rope to get across the yard.

He was thankful that he had finished putting up the lean-to shelters for the cattle out in the field. Hopefully, this storm wouldn't be too hard on them. The shelters would help them survive.

Inside the cozy house, Beatrice and Belle sat in the parlor together. Beatrice played happily with some blocks Joel had made her, but Belle had a hard time concentrating on the mending. Something wasn't right, she could feel it. She sighed, put down her sewing and got up to look out of the window. She could see Joel using the rope to come back to the house. It was already getting dark—night came early in the winter.

"I have an idea! Let's light the candles on the tree and sing some Christmas carols," Belle suggested feigning enthusiasm.

"It won't be as much fun without Ma's piano," Beatrice said.

"But it will still be fun—and wait until you hear Joel's voice. He's got a wonderful baritone," she said cheerfully.

Belle lit the candles on the tree and it looked very festive. Joel entered the parlor after taking off his outerwear and boots and they began singing "Jingle Bells."

He immediately joined in and they spent the next half-hour singing as many Christmas carols as they could remember. Mrs. Ware even came in to sing for a while, then excused herself to get some food ready for the next day.

Joel was still nervous about the candles on the tree so blew them out after they sang a few songs. He threw more logs on the fire and they stood around the roaring blaze, singing their hearts out. Belle tried to stay cheerful but a feeling of dread kept creeping in.

After they exhausted every Christmas song they could think of, Mrs. Ware brought in a surprise. She had made some gingerbread cookies the day before which she had hidden for a special Christmas night treat.

"I wish Pa was here to have one," Beatrice sighed. "He loves gingerbread cookies."

"We will save some for him," Belle assured her. "It will be a nice surprise when he arrives home tomorrow."

They each had several cookies. Mrs. Ware wrapped up the rest then said goodnight and went upstairs.

"It's getting late," Joel warned Beatrice.

"Oh—not yet! Can we open some gifts?" Beatrice begged. "I won't open my present from Ma and Pa. But can I open the present from you?"

"Well, I guess so. It is Christmas, after all," Joel said cheerfully. "And why don't you open my gift, Belle?"

"Only if you will open mine," she replied.

The three opened their gifts, which were wrapped in cheerful scraps of fabric tied with colorful ribbons. Beatrice gasped when she saw the white doll dress that Belle had made her.

"It looks just like your wedding dress and there is even a veil! I bet it will fit Flora perfectly." She took off running upstairs to try it on her doll.

Next, Joel opened his gift. Belle had made fur-lined house slippers. "Your feet are always so cold when you come in at night after chores," she explained. "I was hoping these would help."

"I will wear them every night," he promised, trying them on. "Perfect!" he beamed.

Finally, Belle opened her gift. She nearly fell off her chair when she saw it. It was a gorgeous pearl necklace.

"Joel, this is stunning! But how did you ever afford it?" she asked, amazed.

"I didn't. Ma gave it to me for you. They were her grandmother's pearls, and then her mother's, and then hers. Each of them received it for the birth of their first child. We thought of giving it to you a little early. My part of the gift was to have them re-strung in St. Jo last month. They were so old, we were afraid they would break."

Belle gave him a tremulous smile. "Oh Joel, they are so beautiful. I never thought I would ever have anything so fine. But we should have waited for your Ma to be here."

"No, they are meant to be a gift from a husband to his wife on the birth of their first child. Ma insisted that I give them to you. When they return tomorrow, she will be thrilled to see you wearing them."

"Can you help me try them on?"

The pearls were luminous next to Belle's creamy white skin. The candlelight reflected on the pearls and they glistened like snowdrops. Belle's eyes shone with tears as she gazed at herself in the looking glass.

"Oh, Joel, they are so beautiful. You are so good to me," she whispered.

"Belle, my love," Joel said softly as he turned her around to face him. "You have never looked so beautiful. You positively glow. Pregnancy becomes you, my darling."

They were about to kiss when Beatrice came running down the stairs. She hurled herself at Belle.

"Look at Flora!" she crowed. "The dress fits perfectly! I love it!"

Belle smiled at her. "That's wonderful, Beatrice. I was hoping it would fit. Flora looks just like I did on my wedding day."

"Oh no, you were much prettier," Beatrice whispered. "But don't tell Flora!"

"Well, it's bedtime for you and Flora," Joel announced. "I'll go back outside to check on the stock again—it's finally stopped snowing. It looks like we got at least a foot."

"When will Ma and Pa be home?" Beatrice asked, voice quavering.

"Tomorrow sometime, I'm sure," Joel assured her. "They will have to go slowly with all the snow."

"OK," Beatrice said, and she yawned.

"Come on, I'll tuck you in," said Belle to Beatrice. Joel made his way back outside.

Beatrice brushed her teeth using her tooth cloth, washed her face, put on her nightgown, and was asleep almost immediately, hugging her doll.

Belle extinguished the lights and then went upstairs to their bedroom. She undressed and washed herself quickly, leaving her new pearls on. After a while, she heard Joel coming up the stairs. When he entered the room, she was standing at the window looking at the snow. She was wearing the white gown from her wedding night even though it was a bit tight.

"It is so pretty out there with all the snow," she whispered.

"Yes, but really cold," Joel answered, taking off his clothes. "I feel like I need to warm up."

Joel walked over to her and kissed her ardently. He slipped the gown off of her. They made love with the pearls still around her neck.

Afterwards, Joel said, "I'm afraid every time I see those pearls on you, I will picture this moment in the candlelight with the pearls glowing against your naked skin. How will I ever be able to contain myself?"

Belle smiled at him, then took off her pearls and got into a warm flannel gown. As she cuddled up to Joel she whispered, "Do you really think our folks are all right?"

"I hope so," he said grimly. "Unfortunately, I believe the storm was coming from the west so if they were still riding fast, it would have hit them first. It got pretty intense quickly. I believe that they were probably about thirty minutes from town, so I am a bit worried. But old Mr. Hadley's farm is on the way and not far off the road. Perhaps they stopped there if it got too bad."

"I pray it is so," Belle said quietly.

TWENTY

Waking just before dawn, Joel slipped out of bed and threw on his clothes quietly, so as not to disturb Belle. He had double the chores with his farmhand away for Christmas. George was set to return later in the day, but on this morning, Joel was on his own.

Joel walked out into the bitterly cold dawn. His dogs Rex and Pal barked excitedly when they saw him, running around in circles. The sun was about to rise, and Joel could see it was going to be a clear day. He stopped for a moment and gazed at the pink sky on the glistening snow. It was so beautiful.

Inside the barn while he milked the cow, he made a decision. He would take the cutter to town to pick up their parents. He was not sure William could make it through all the snow in his carriage.

Joel pulled the cutter out from the back of the barn so it would be ready to go. He could fit the four adults in, it was a two-seater. It would be cold—it was not enclosed—but they could bundle up and be warm enough.

After feeding the livestock, he came into the kitchen and was glad to see Belle up, making breakfast. He sat down, ate quickly, and told her of his plan.

"I wish I could go," she sighed. "I'll just be here, fretting and worrying. But I can't leave Beatrice."

"I wouldn't want you to come in any case, not in your condition," he replied. "It's cold."

Joel dressed as warmly as he could, with extra scarves covering his

"

face, and put two pairs of socks in his boots. He put on warm mittens. Belle had hard-boiled some eggs that morning so he could put them in his mittened hands when they got cold, at least for a while—then he could eat them. He found a few wool blankets to cover up with as well.

"It should warm up a bit," he said, squinting at the sky. "But let me have the extra scarves, in case our parents need them."

After he was ready, he kissed Belle and told her not to worry. "I'll be back before you know it," he said cheerfully.

But he had a bad feeling inside. Looking at Belle's face, he could see that she did too.

Blue was able to go fast in the snow as it was already hard-packed. They skimmed along, making good time. Joel kept looking left and right, not sure exactly what he was looking for.

After he passed the Hadley farm, he could see something on the side of the road, way off in the distance. His heart sank.

His father-in-law's carriage was overturned. One of his horses lay in the ditch, dead. Joel saw a strangely shaped mound of snow a few feet away. He dug it out and found his father-in-law William, who had obviously been thrown from the carriage.

On the other side of the carriage was another shape, covered in snow. With his heart in his mouth, he dug out Mary. It looked like she had also been badly hurt and had died from her injuries.

But where was Ma? He could see some faint indentations, like a trail covered by more snow. Perhaps she had walked until she had found shelter? In a state of shock, he followed the trail, wading through the deep snow for a time, and then he saw that awful mound of snow again.

His ma had frozen to death, which was clear. She had probably tried to find shelter, but would have been unable to see anything in the blizzard. With tears streaming down his face, he picked up her frozen body and carried it back to the broken carriage, and laid it there. He would need to get help to bring their bodies back home.

Joel rode as fast as he could to Hadley's farm. Mr. Hadley and his son jumped on their horses and rode to the scene of the accident, where they helped him to place the bodies in Joel's cutter.

Joel felt sick to his stomach. How could he go back home with these three bodies? This would kill Belle.

"I'll go into town and let the sheriff know," Mr. Hadley said sadly. "I'm sure folks will be out there soon to help you prepare the bodies, to console and pray with all of you. We will need to ask the coffin-maker to come out as well. Of course, you will have to wait until spring to bury them. The ground is too frozen. But perhaps we can have a prayer service at church tomorrow or the next day."

Joel said nothing. He could think of no response.

Looking at Joel's face, Mr. Hadley told his son to ride back and ask his mother to come out to the road.

"She can ride with you back to your home. Likely she is getting ready to do so anyway," he said.

The three men left. Mr. Hadley rode toward town at a fast pace. Joel drove Blue slowly toward his home with the bodies in the back of the cutter.

Tears coursed down Joel's face. What would he tell his wife? What would happen to Beatrice? Soon he came to the Hadley place and stopped.

Jean Hadley climbed in the cutter and put her hand on Joel's arm.

"Joel, cry your tears now. When you reach home, you will need to be strong for Belle and her sister. Belle being pregnant is particularly worrying, as shocks like this have been known to put women into early labor from time to time. You will need to pull yourself together and help her to be calm."

"How will I tell Belle? How can I tell Beatrice that her parents are gone? She's only eleven years old. And how can I bear it as well? My mother froze to death," he sobbed aloud.

"You must bear it. You are the man of the house. You must comfort and calm Belle and her sister. You must be strong," she said firmly.

They rode in silence after that.

When they approached the house, Joel pulled the cutter into the barn. Mrs. Hadley helped him to unhitch the horses. They quickly closed the barn door and walked slowly to the house.

They found Belle and Mrs. Ware in the kitchen, washing one of Joel's shirts and other items of clothing in the washtub. Beatrice was sitting on the floor, playing with her doll.

"How are you back already?" Belle said in astonishment. "And is that you, Mrs. Hadley? Where are our parents?"

Joel said nothing.

"Let's go sit in the parlor, and we will talk," Jean Hadley suggested.

"I'll just put the kettle on," Mrs. Ware said, sensing that something terrible had happened.

A feeling of dread came over Belle. Something was wrong.

They all sat down in the parlor, including Beatrice, who looked puzzled but stayed silent. Joel sat next to Belle on the settee and took her hand. The parlor still had the Christmas tree up, with presents under the tree. When Joel looked at the tree, he felt himself starting to tear up.

He pulled himself together, cleared his throat and began, speaking softly. "Our parents had an accident on the way to church yesterday. Something made the horses veer off the road and into a ditch. The buggy overturned. Our parents were all killed."

Belle's face went white. But Beatrice's face went red.

"You are a liar!" Beatrice shouted. "My parents can't be dead. They were going to church!"

"I'm sorry to say that it is true," Joel said, trying to hold back a sob. He looked at Belle, who was just staring straight ahead, not moving. Beatrice continued to scream, so Jean Hadley went to try and comfort her.

"Darling, are you alright? Speak to me," he whispered.

Belle didn't answer. Beatrice threw herself at Belle, sobbing and crying. Belle still sat there, not moving.

Jean got up to make some tea with plenty of sugar for the shock. She suggested that Joel take the girls upstairs and get them comfortable and warm. After Beatrice had calmed down a bit, Joel took them upstairs, undressed Belle and put them both in their bed together, covering them up with quilts. Beatrice continued to cry more quietly, but Joel was worried about Belle. She was still just staring straight ahead.

Jean came up with three cups of sugary tea. She sat next to Beatrice and encouraged her to drink the tea. Joel sat next to Belle and got her to take a few sips. He whispered for them to try to sleep a bit. Obediently, they both lay down and closed their eyes. Joel sat watching them while he sipped his cup of tea. Tears streamed down his face as he looked at them both. How would they ever cope?

After a while, Jean motioned for him to come downstairs. He checked that they were both asleep and followed her, wiping his eyes. Mrs. Ware was standing at the washtub, continuing to scrub the clothes (it was wash day) with tears streaming down her face.

"When does your farmhand arrive?" Jean asked. "I was going to see if he would go get the Frasers to come over."

Joel shook his head. "Not for a while," he said.

"Well, I'm sure Belle's aunt is on her way out here. Someone can go get the Frasers once folks start arriving. We will need Mildred Fraser's help with the laying out. Now Mrs. Ware and I are going to get some food together, and I will need your help. Can you put a big kettle of water onto the stove? We will need some hot water," she said.

Joel walked around in shock, doing whatever Jean asked him to do, trying not to think. After a while she sent him up to check on the girls. They were both still asleep.

He wished he could sleep. The vision of their parents' faces in death kept returning to him. It was all he could do to not just break down and cry. But Jean was right. He needed to be the rock right now.

He was so tired he could barely stand. Jean came up the stairs.

"Why don't you go lie down for a bit in Beatrice's room?" she whispered. "I'll come get you when folks arrive and when the girls wake."

Joel nodded numbly. He walked into the room Beatrice had been sleeping in, took his boots off, and lay down on the bed. He fell asleep almost instantly.

The next few days dragged by. Belle had a hard time keeping her spirits up, even though she knew it was important to do so for both Beatrice's and Joel's sakes. She also suspected that it was unhealthy for the baby that she cried so much. But she couldn't seem to stop. She really just wanted to go to bed and sleep all day.

Mrs. Ware decided to move in with them. "I need to be with you and Beatrice just like your Ma would expect," she told Belle. "Plus you need the help, I can see." It was obvious that Belle was beyond cooking, laundry, or doing housework right now.

Since her parents' deaths, Belle had done little but sit and stare out the window. She spent some time with Beatrice each day and tried to help with the housework, but her heart wasn't in it. She felt exhausted, cried most of the day. She just wanted to sleep.

But each time she awoke from sleep, the tragedy would hit her all over again --fresh grief would overwhelm her. She spent her waking hours in a daze, walking around with a heavy heart.

Joel too was grieving, but tried not to let it show around Belle. One night he looked around the dinner table and realized they were three orphans, all living together. The thought made him feel so downhearted. But he needed to be strong.

His mother Anna had always wanted grandchildren. She had been as excited as Belle and Joel were for the new baby. Belle and Anna had talked about how to care for the baby almost every day. Belle's mother was also excited, and had sewn and crocheted baskets of baby clothing and blankets. Even William's eyes sparkled when they talked about the baby. But they would never get to hold their first grandchild.

Like Belle, Beatrice cried a lot at first. But she had the resiliency of the young and could be distracted with little things, like a new chick hatching, or a visit to the Frasers' house.

Belle was another matter.

One morning a couple of weeks after the tragedy, Mrs. Ware came outside to find Joel in the barn. He was milking the cow, a job Belle used to do—before she became this empty shell.

"Mr. Joel, I'm real worried about Belle and that new baby," she said. "It's not good for a woman in her condition to sit and stare or cry all day.

She's gonna have a long hard labor without her mama at her side. We gotta cheer her up somehow."

Joel sighed. "I'm worried too. But I don't know what to do. I'm not myself, either."

"Hmmpf," Mrs. Ware said. "Maybe you go over and ask Mrs. Fraser what to do? She might have a few ideas."

"That's a good idea. Maybe I'll take Beatrice over there. They keep asking us to let her spend a few days with them. I wish I could take Belle, but I don't want to chance it with her time so near."

"Well, that's fine," she said. "I'll keep Belle busy, don't you fret. But you need to come up with something to perk her up."

"Thank you, Mrs. Ware, I will. I don't know how we could cope without you."

"I know. And I won't ever leave Belle and Beatrice. I owe that to their ma," she said and then went back inside.

The next day Joel and Beatrice made their way to the Frasers.

As they pulled up to the Fraser house, Mary and Sally came spilling out onto the porch. The girls whisked Beatrice upstairs to show her some dresses they had altered for her, and Joel came inside the kitchen to warm up and talk to Mildred and Ebenezer Fraser.

Mildred brewed Joel a hot cup of coffee and the three of them sat down. Joel explained his concerns about Belle.

"Oh my," sighed Mildred. "I'm not surprised. This is always a tough time for women anyway, right before the first baby is born. But to lose both mothers on top of it—no wonder she is so sad."

"She just wants to lie in bed and sleep all day," Joel said. "I was hoping you could help me think of a way to lift her spirits."

"I imagine you need your spirits lifted as well, young man," remarked Ebenezer.

"Well, yes," Joel admitted. "I try not to let it show in front of Belle, but I have some tough nights, that's for sure."

"What are you doing about the Westlake's farm?" Ebenezer asked.

"Their foreman and the farmhands are taking care of it all right now.

I'll have to go out there sometime in the spring to get it ready to sell, I guess," he said glumly.

"Well, I have an idea," Mildred said. "Let's throw a baby quilting party for Belle. I'll have Amos take me into town and I will invite all the ladies we know. Do you think we could pull this off in five days?"

"I don't know if Belle is up to a party right now," Joel said hesitantly.

"It's more like a baby welcoming, advice giving, get-together. We used to have those all the time, but somehow it fell out of fashion. We will make a couple of quilts for the baby, talk about motherhood, and have fun. We'll bring all the food and supplies. You will just need to supply Belle."

"Well, all right. If you think that could help," he said dubiously. "But I'm going to wait and tell her right before. Otherwise, she will fret about it too much."

"We will tell Beatrice, but swear her to secrecy," Mildred said. "She can help us with the preparations. It will do her good to think about something other than her sadness. But now, as for you—"

"I have an idea," Ebenezer Fraser said. "I'll come to the party with a surprise for you, Joel."

"That is so kind," Joel said. "I'm truly grateful for the help."

Five days later, Joel came into the kitchen where Mrs. Ware was fixing breakfast. The good weather had held, so it looked like the party would be on.

Beatrice was still at the Frasers'. Belle had asked about her, but Joel assured her that she was having fun and that the Frasers would bring her back sometime today.

Belle sat listlessly at the table picking at her food. Joel looked at Mrs. Ware, and she nodded.

"Darling," Joel began. "Why don't you finish your breakfast and go upstairs and put on your Sunday best? We have a surprise for you."

Belle gave Joel a curious look. "You know my crinoline doesn't fit me anymore. I'm too big. What is the surprise?"

Mrs. Ware piped up. "I let out one of Anna's nice dresses for you. Now don't fuss, she would be so happy for you to wear it. Let's go upstairs and try it on."

"What is going on?" Belle asked, looking at them both.

"We are having a baby quilting get-together with Mildred and some of the other ladies from town," Joel explained.

"I'm not ready for that!" Belle gasped. "I haven't even washed my hair in weeks, and I look a fright. I can't have a party. I'm too sad."

"Now honey, don't you worry," said Mrs. Ware gently. "Mr. Joel can clean up this kitchen and you and me are going to get you all fixed up. Let's go on upstairs now."

"We don't even have any food!" Belle protested. "And is the parlor even clean?"

"We got some food I've hidden away and the ladies are bringing more, don't you worry," promised Mrs. Ware. "Mr. Joel will clean that parlor, too—won't you, Mr. Joel?"

"Yes, ma'am. Now go get ready," Joel said firmly.

Belle walked upstairs with Mrs. Ware, grumbling all the way. After about an hour, she came downstairs. She wore one of his mother's favorite dresses, with her pearls around her neck.

Joel whistled when he saw her. "Darling, you look beautiful," he said. "Now, let's go check the parlor and you can let me know what else I need to do there."

Beatrice arrived with the Frasers shortly after, in a new dress they had made for her. Her eyes were sparkling. After hugging Belle and Joel, she ran into the parlor with Mary and Sally to put up some handmade decorations.

A few minutes later, ten more ladies arrived. They all exclaimed at how beautiful Belle looked, and brought in more food than they could have possibly eaten. Mr. Fraser and Amos had brought some extra chairs from their house and the ladies sat in the parlor, creating a couple of baby quilts with some of the fabrics from both Belle's and Joel's mothers' dresses. Mrs. Ware had thoughtfully gathered some of those once she heard about the quilting party.

There was advice given on controlling the pain during labor, taking care of a newborn, nursing the baby, and even how to keep her husband from feeling neglected as she was focusing most of her attention on the baby.

"They tell you to wait three months, but if you do that you will have a very unhappy husband," one of the older ladies, Mrs. Cane, whispered to Belle. "You can do it as soon as you feel healed. And you won't get in the family way if you're nursing!"

"Now that's not true," Mildred Fraser said. "Why do you think my Amos and Mary are less than a year apart? I was nursing!"

"Ma!" Mary and Sally exclaimed, horrified.

"Very unusual, that," Mrs. Cane sniffed. "Anyway, you got to keep him happy in some way. That always seemed the easiest way to me!"

All the ladies giggled, along with Belle. She realized that she had not laughed since Christmas day.

"What are you talking about?" Beatrice asked.

"Never mind, honey," Belle said. "We will talk about that when you get older."

For Joel's sake, Mr. Fraser had brought both wood and a sketch on how to make the rocking chair. The three men started making it together; Joel would finish it by himself for Belle. It was a comfort to Joel to sit and talk with them as they worked together on the chair.

A few hours later, Joel and Belle stood in the doorway, waving goodbye to their guests.

"I feel lighter somehow," she sighed. "Oh, thank you Joel! It's just what I needed. And I can't wait to sit in my new rocking chair."

"Well, it's gonna be awhile before that's finished." He smiled in relief. "Now let's go eat some more of that food. It is delicious."

TWENTY-ONE

Belle

- February 1891 -

Belle stood at the window, staring out at the storm. It was yet another blizzard. They were having a hard winter again this year. Joel was out in the barn, tending to the livestock. Beatrice was sitting at the kitchen table, working on her sums. They did not take her to school in town that day because of the storm.

Blizzard weather made Belle feel so sad. She pictured her parents driving in the blizzard and crashing in the ditch. Had they suffered? There was no way of knowing. She hoped not.

Belle looked down at her pregnant belly, rubbing it gently. How sad she was that neither of their mothers would ever know their grandchild. Both mothers had talked so excitedly about the baby. They had sewn so many baby clothes, blankets, diapers, and had promised to help her care for him or her.

Before she died, Joel's mother had told Joel to bring the cradle down from the attic for their baby, the same one Joel had slept in. It was also the same one his father had slept in—Joel's grandfather had made it. But Joel had not brought it down yet. It was almost as if he had lost interest in the baby. He never talked about the baby anymore, although he still worked on the rocking chair every night.

Of course, they were all still sad. The party had helped, but the long winter days and nights did not. They tried to act somewhat cheerful for Beatrice's sake, but it was hard. Beatrice had struggled at first, but seemed to adjust to living at Belle and Joel's house pretty quickly. She still cried for her mother and father sometimes, but those times were getting fewer.

It helped to have Mrs. Ware around. She talked about their mother which helped them to move through their grief.

Belle still cried most nights, usually after Joel was asleep. She suspected Joel cried when he was in the barn sometimes, as his eyes were often red when he came inside.

Belle knew that discovering the bodies had been hard on Joel. He had nightmares. He wouldn't tell her what they were about, but she was pretty sure that he was reliving that gruesome discovery in his dreams.

She sighed. It was hard to be excited about the baby with so much sadness in her life. But she hoped that once their sweet baby was here, her heart would heal, and Joel's too.

Joel came stamping into the house. "It's pretty bad out there," he said, unwinding his scarf. "I've put the rope up between the house and barn, as I don't see this letting up very soon. When will we have supper? I have told George to come in as soon as he finishes his chores."

"Supper is almost ready," Belle said. "Why don't you go wash up, and you can have some hot tea while I finish baking the biscuits? We'll make some tea for George too. He will probably need to sleep in the house tonight, won't he? That seems safer."

"Yes," Joel replied. "I have told him as much. I'll go wash up." He hurried upstairs.

Mrs. Ware made the tea and Belle put the biscuits in the oven. She had Beatrice set the table. George came in, and she sent him upstairs to wash up as well.

At dinner Joel talked about a new calf their cow Bessie would have in the spring.

"Can I name her?" Beatrice asked. "I can help take care of her, too!"

"Of course," Joel smiled at her. "Did you finish your sums? I don't think you will have school tomorrow, but you must stay caught up. I can help you tomorrow with them."

"Well, I hate sums. Pa said they were so important, but I don't agree." Realizing what she had said, her eyes filled with tears. "I miss him," she said quietly.

"Come over and help me dish up the soup, Beatrice," Belle said, trying to distract her. They had both cried so many tears over the past weeks. Sometimes Belle felt like they would never stop crying.

After dinner, the four of them went into the parlor while Mrs. Ware did the dishes. Belle was finishing a baby blanket her mother had started while Joel continued to read *The Adventures of Huckleberry Finn*. His mother had given the book to him for Christmas. She had also given him *Treasure Island*. She had written a note to him on the flyleaf, which he read every time he opened the book:

> *To my dear son, Joel Casper Watson,*
> *Christmas, 1890.*
> *May you always love reading!*
> *With love from*
> *your devoted mother.*

Beatrice sat on the floor, playing with her doll and George sat at the window, looking out at the storm. Mrs. Ware said goodnight after finishing the dishes and went upstairs.

After a while George remarked, "I think it's letting up. Should I go out and check on the stock once more?"

"Certainly, if you don't mind. It's getting late anyhow. We will have a big day tomorrow, so I might turn in. What about you, ladies?" Joel asked.

"All right," yawned Beatrice. "Will you tuck me in, Belle?" she asked. Beatrice had asked Belle to tuck her into bed every night since their parents had died.

"Of course, sweetheart. Go get on your nightgown and I'll be in your room to say prayers and tell you a story in a few minutes."

After she tucked her sister in, Belle got into her own bed. Joel was still awake, staring at the ceiling.

"Are you all right, my dear?" she asked softly. "I know this is hard. I'm sad, too."

"It's these nightmares," he confessed. "They wear me out. I wish they would stop."

"Why don't we focus on the baby and see if that helps?" Belle suggested. "I think it helps me a little when I look forward, not backwards. Maybe you could bring the cradle down from the attic tomorrow and I will prepare it for the baby. What do you think?"

"Of course. I have been meaning to do that. I just get sad every time I realize that our mothers will never see our child, so I guess I have avoided it."

Belle snuggled close to him. "That makes me sad too. But I know our mothers wouldn't want us to feel sad, only happy for our baby."

"That's true," he sighed.

Belle kissed him passionately and they came together with an intensity they had not felt since the deaths of their parents. Joel fell asleep immediately after their lovemaking and, for the first time in a month, he had no nightmares.

The next day Joel spent some time in the attic and found the cradle, a basket for the baby to sleep downstairs, and even his grandmother's rocking chair. He put the old, comfortable rocking chair in the parlor so Belle could have a pleasant place to nurse the baby when downstairs. He had finally finished his rocking chair, which he had put in their room.

Belle cleaned the furniture and began to work on a new goose down mattress for the cradle. With Beatrice's help they assembled all of the baby clothes and blankets and put them in the cozy little nursery, which was next door to Belle and Joel's room.

By the end of the day, Belle felt relieved. The baby could be born in a week or less, and she had been worried that they were not ready. Now she could relax a bit. She just needed to wait for labor to begin, and she would be on her way to motherhood.

The midwife, Mrs. Grant, came by the next day, examined Belle and told her the baby could come any time.

"How quickly will you be able to get here?" Joel asked anxiously.

"First babies don't usually come quickly," she replied. "But once Belle starts having pains or if her waters break, jump in your cutter and come get me. Could your farmhand go get a neighbor to stay with Belle?"

"Oh yes," answered Belle. "He can go get Mildred Fraser."

"That's wonderful," said Mrs. Grant. "Mildred will know just what to do. Your housekeeper Mrs. Ware can help too. I will see you soon, my dear. Get lots of rest—you will need it."

The days went by slowly. Belle was getting more and more uncomfortable. Beatrice was too anxious to leave her, so Belle taught her lessons at home.

Finally, on a sunny February day, Belle woke up with back pain.

"Did you overdo it yesterday?" Joel asked anxiously.

"No, I don't think I did too much," Belle answered. "We did the washing yesterday, but Beatrice and Mrs. Ware helped with all the heavy lifting—ooooh! That feels funny. It's like a tightening in my belly. Joel, this could be labor pains."

"I better go get the midwife!" he said in a panicky voice. "I'll send George to get Mrs. Fraser right now. Don't get up!"

"Joel, calm down. The midwife said I could have pains for many hours. You and George go take care of the animals. Mrs. Ware and I will fix some breakfast, and after you eat, you can go," she said in a soothing voice.

"Are you sure? All right, but we will hurry." Joel threw on his clothes and clattered down the stairs and outside.

Belle sighed, got dressed slowly, not really feeling any labor pains until after quite a few minutes.

She woke Beatrice, who was very excited to hear the news, and they fixed a nice breakfast of flapjacks, bacon, and potatoes.

Joel and George came in noisily, sat down, and ate in record time.

"I'll be back as soon as I can. George, you need to ride over and get Mrs. Fraser. Beatrice, stay with Belle every second!" Joel came over, kissed Belle, and ran out the door. Every twenty minutes or so, Belle would feel a bit of her belly tightening and some discomfort, but it wasn't too bad.

After an hour or two, Mrs. Ware shooed Belle upstairs. She wanted her to get in the bed which was ready for the birth and wait.

But Belle could not stand to lie in the bed and wait for the pains. Instead, she walked around the upstairs hall, bending over and breathing fast when she felt a labor pain. Beatrice walked right next to her, holding her hand.

Mildred Fraser arrived and a few hours later, so did the midwife. By this time, Belle was in bed as her water had broken. Her pains were getting more and more intense. She was relieved to see Joel and Mrs. Grant. Mr. Fraser came over to sit with Joel.

Belle wished so much that her mother could be there. She tried not to cry for her, but when the worst pains came, she did.

Mildred Fraser was so kind. "Your mother is here in spirit," she said quietly, mopping her brow.

"I'm here too," Beatrice said.

Mrs. Ware realized Belle was going into transition. She gave Mildred Fraser a look, nodding her head at Beatrice.

"Beatrice, why don't you go sit with Joel?" Mildred suggested. "I imagine he could use your support."

"Is that alright Belle?" Beatrice asked anxiously.

Through a great deal of effort, Belle was able to smile at her. "Yes, darling. Go sit with Joel and tell him I am OK," she said in a cheerful voice.

Beatrice went downstairs and then finally it was time to push. After just a few minutes, her baby boy was born. When Joel heard the baby cry, he bounded up the stairs, two at a time.

"Come meet your son," Belle said proudly when he entered the room.

Joel held his son and looked at Belle with tears in his eyes. Then Mildred Fraser took him from Joel, cleaned him up and gave him to Belle to nurse.

"Did it hurt awful bad?" Joel asked Belle. "I could hear you cry out some. Beatrice was scared, but I told her it was normal."

"Yes, it did hurt," Belle admitted. "Where is Beatrice?"

"Here I am," Beatrice said shyly from the door.

"Come see your little nephew." Belle smiled at her. "I hope you will help me to take care of him."

"Oh, I will!" Beatrice said with shining eyes as she watched Belle nurse the baby. "Does he have blue eyes like me? How come he doesn't have any hair?"

They all laughed.

" Don't worry—it will grow," Mrs. Ware said. "You didn't have any hair to speak of when you was born either."

"What are we calling this little man?" asked Mildred Fraser.

"We will call him LeRoy Gilbert William Watson," Belle said, beaming at Joel.

"Hello, LeRoy," Joel said softly.

"I like that name LeRoy," Beatrice said. "How did you think of it?"

"That was Belle's first Pa's name," Mrs. Ware said to Beatrice. "He was such a good man."

"And Gilbert was my Pa's name, so this little guy is named after all of his grandpas," Joel said, hugging Beatrice. "He's going to be a very special little boy."

"And I'm going to be the best aunt ever!" Beatrice said.

"Maybe you all should get some supper started," Mrs. Grant suggested when she saw Belle beginning to strain again. "Mr. Joel, don't you need to see about the livestock?"

"Yes ma'am," Joel said.

Everyone but Mildred and Mrs. Grant scooted out of the room as Belle delivered the afterbirth. The two women finished cleaning Belle and LeRoy. Then they changed the bed linens around Belle and made her comfortable.

After everyone left the room, Belle smiled down at her new son. "Welcome to the world, little one," she whispered.

TWENTY-TWO

- 1892 -

As Joel rode out to check on the cattle, he thought about how far they had come the past year. They finally sold Belle's parents' farm. Belle and Joel put half the money in the bank for Beatrice and used the other half to buy more cattle, other livestock, and some new farm equipment. The improvements helped to dig the farm out of a financial hole and for the first time, it was making money.

Joel was grateful for the financial boon but would have traded it all to have their parents back again. Every time he thought of them, the gruesome sight of their deaths would flash before his eyes. He still had nightmares sometimes. On top of that, he regretted spending those two years away from his mother, now that she was gone. He felt so sad that she would never even meet her grandson.

Sometimes he wondered if this sorrow he felt would ever go away. But then, he would look at Belle and LeRoy and realize how fortunate they really were. It was impossible to stay sad when such a happy little boy was in the house.

Beatrice still missed her parents, but she had school and friends to distract her. She now lived in town with Belle's Aunt Irene when school was in session—it was just too far to take her into town every day. She missed her family—especially LeRoy—but it made everyone's life so much easier. Belle's aunt and uncle adored Beatrice and it was nice for her to have some friends in town to play with. She came back out to the farm most weekends.

Belle's days were filled with taking care of LeRoy, washing clothes, cleaning, and cooking, along with Mrs. Ware's help. Once they sold her parents' farm, they were finally able to pay Mrs. Ware a decent wage. They had hired Zeke, another farmhand, to help George. Now Joel was able to spend more time with Belle, even helping with LeRoy some of the time.

Joel loved spending time with LeRoy. He was such a happy baby! He had started walking at the age of one year. His first word was "Dada." Joel loved to chase LeRoy around and wrestle with him. They spent many happy times playing together, with Belle giggling from the sidelines.

The beginning of June started off dry once again. Joel planned to buy hay for his cattle the next winter, as he knew he could not depend on the prairie grasses anymore. He had planted hay the year before, but decided to rest the land and buy it this year.

Joel had spent some time at the farmers' meetings at the Grange in Tethertown. At one of the meetings, an expert on farming from the Missouri Ag College suggested growing hay every other year. This new theory was that the soil needed to rest. Farmers were starting to realize their old way of life, with the cattle fattening up in the summer on prairie grasses, was over. They needed hay to feed their cattle all year round.

After the meeting, Joel had decided that he would start to grow more hay, beginning next year. He had another field he could use; he just had to get it ready. He would need to clean up the area, work the soil, and remove any debris. He was willing to try anything. They did not want to lose any more cattle.

Standing outside, looking at the field he needed to work on for next year's planting, Joel thought of Belle. He was worried about her. Belle had not been feeling well lately. She seemed more tired than usual. She could not seem to eat very much. It finally dawned on him that she must be with child again. That was exactly how she had felt when she was pregnant with LeRoy.

Joel jumped on his horse and trotted to the house. He ran inside but then found Belle in the backyard, wringing out their laundry on the mangle by the clothesline.

"I thought you were going to have Mrs. Ware do the washing. Here, let me help with that," he said, walking up to her. Joel grabbed the sheet she had been wringing out and took over.

"You don't have to help!" Belle exclaimed. "I am doing this because I would rather be outside. I asked Mrs. Ware to cook instead of doing the laundry. I don't like being in the kitchen on these warm days. She said she would do the ironing, which you know I hate doing. I swear that iron must weigh 10 pounds, Anyway, don't you need to go work on the new hay field? Isn't that what you told me this morning?"

"That can wait. I like to help my beautiful wife," Joel said. "I always used to love helping Ma wring out the laundry."

After they finished wringing out the clothes and hanging them to dry, Joel took Belle's hands, looked her in the eyes and asked, "So, do you think LeRoy is going to have a little sister or a little brother?"

Belle looked down. "I didn't want to tell you until I was sure," she answered.

"When will you know for sure?" he asked eagerly.

"I'll go to town next month and meet with Doctor Gordon," she answered. "It's still early days."

Just then they heard LeRoy waking up from his nap upstairs.

"Why don't you sit under the tree and relax?" Joel suggested. "I'll go get our boy."

Before she could answer, Joel sprinted inside. Belle sat under the walnut tree and leaned her head back. Feeling the gentle breeze, she relaxed and closed her eyes.

Sometime later, she opened her eyes, realizing she had fallen asleep. *I must be with child, to have fallen asleep so easily,* she thought. She got up slowly and went out to the barn where LeRoy and Joel were having a good time, chasing the chickens.

. . .

Their daughter arrived six months later. LeRoy grew bigger and their new baby girl was an easy, placid baby. They named her Laura Anna, after Belle's grandmother and Joel's mother. Everyone doted on the sweet little girl. She had brown eyes and chestnut colored hair.

Life on the farm was hard work, but filled with happiness every day. Joel and Belle had never lost the passion between them. Life was good.

One April morning in 1893, Belle brought up the green apples, stored in the cellar. She was going to make a green apple pie, one of Joel's favorites. Leaving the basket of apples on the floor, she went outside with Mrs. Ware to take the laundry down. It looked like rain.

There was a soft spring breeze. Belle took her time, savoring the end of winter and the coming of warmer weather. After a while, it began to sprinkle.

When she came back inside, she found LeRoy on the floor, eating the green apples. It looked like he had eaten almost five of them—quite a lot for a two-year-old.

"No, no, LeRoy!" she chastised him. "Those are for Daddy's pie." Luckily, she had enough in the basket that it made little difference.

They had the delicious pie that night, with LeRoy having two pieces and then asking for another.

"No more, LeRoy. This boy is going to get sick to his stomach," Belle said. "Too many green apples!"

In the middle of the night, she could hear LeRoy crying. When she went into the nursery, she found him lying in his own mess, looking sickly. Belle went to clean him up and then he began vomiting.

Oh dear, she thought. *All those green apples!*

LeRoy continued to have diarrhea and vomiting throughout the night. Finally, she woke Joel.

"You'd better get the doctor," she said. "He's getting pretty glassy-eyed and lethargic. And his heart seems to be beating very fast."

Joel jumped on his horse and rode as quickly as he could to town. Doctor Gordon was not at home, as he was with a sick elderly patient. By the time Joel found him, the sun was up.

"Get as much water down him as you can." the doctor advised. "Small sips. I'll be out to evaluate him as soon as I eat something. Keep him away from the baby."

Joel raced home and by then, LeRoy was even worse. They tried getting water down his throat, but he would take very little. Before long, he was feverish.

By the time Doctor Gordon arrived, Belle and Joel were very worried. The doctor evaluated him and said they should continue to try to get him to take sips of water. He gave them some medicine to bring down his fever.

Joel walked the doctor outside. Doctor Gordon turned to Joel. "I have seen this before. Some think it has to do with eating too many green apples, but I don't know. It could also be cholera. There have been a few cases in town. Has LeRoy been in town lately? Some say cholera can travel in water. I'm starting to suspect there is a water source in town that is carrying it."

"We were in town a week or so ago, picking up Beatrice. We all drank from the well, it was a hot day. But I feel fine!" Joel protested.

"There's no telling why some get sick and why some don't. The next twenty-four hours are crucial. Give him cool baths and keep trying to get him to drink water. I'll be back tonight."

"Could he die?" Joel asked fearfully.

"I won't lie to you. He is not out of the woods yet. He is small and severely dehydrated already. If he goes into convulsions, he could die."

Joel turned white. He went inside and got the tub ready to give his son a cooling bath.

The next few hours were excruciating. LeRoy did not improve. He had terrible stomach cramps and a fever. He was getting weaker. Joel sent George to get Beatrice in town and bring her home.

When the doctor returned, he sat with LeRoy and then told Belle and Joel to stay by LeRoy's side. "I don't think he will make it through the night," he said sadly.

The scared parents sat with their son, prayed, and talked to him, holding him in their arms. Beatrice came in and sang to him, Mrs. Ware brought in food that no one could eat.

Around midnight, LeRoy went into a convulsion and died.

Belle screamed and fell to the ground. Joel wailed aloud. Beatrice came running into the room, crying.

Joel had sent for Mildred Fraser a few minutes after the doctor had returned. When she heard the wailing, she came upstairs and sat with them. Mrs. Ware took Beatrice back to bed. After a while, Doctor Gordon sent the parents to go to sleep. Mildred carried LeRoy's body downstairs. With tears streaming down their faces, Mrs. Ware and Mildred bathed and prepared the baby boy for the funeral and burial, which would take place in two days.

The coffin maker in town came out the next morning with a child-sized pine coffin. Joel placed his little boy in the box and carried it to the parlor. All day, friends and neighbors came to call. The women brought food and sat with Belle and Beatrice, trying to console them. The men helped Joel with the farm work and then came to sit with him.

It was a dreadful day. Belle was numb, staring into space. The women took care of Laura, bringing her to Belle to nurse. Joel sat on the porch, staring ahead wordlessly with red eyes. Beatrice just cried silently, tears slipping down her cheeks. Only sweet little six-month-old Laura was happy and smiling.

The next morning, they loaded the little coffin into their wagon and took it to the church.

The funeral service was heartbreaking. When the choir sang "Abide with Me," Both Joel and Belle broke down and cried. Beatrice cried so hard she could barely stand.

At the graveside, Belle could hardly make herself throw the dirt on the coffin. After all the mourners left, she stayed sitting by the open grave until Joel led her away.

The next few weeks were agonizing. Everything reminded them of their darling boy. Belle didn't have the luxury of sleeping the miserable days away like when her parents died. She had Laura to take care of. In many ways, that helped her to cope more than anything.

A few weeks later while sitting at the kitchen table shelling peas, Beatrice asked, "Do you think Mama is taking care of LeRoy in heaven?"

Belle's eyes filled with tears. "Yes, I do. It is a great comfort to me."

CHAPTER TWENTY-TWO

"Then Mama and Pa get to be with him now—Miss Anna too?"

"Yes, sweetheart. He is well loved there, just like he was here," Belle said sadly. "God loved him so much he had to bring him home. But we will always miss him."

Joel was standing outside the door, tears in his eyes, listening to his wife.

"Ma, take care of our boy," he whispered in prayer.

That night Belle and Joel made love for the first time since LeRoy had died. They both cried afterwards in each other's arms.

"I hope God sends us another baby soon," Belle whispered.

"Me too," Joel said. No child would ever take their sweet boy's place, but a new baby would help them all.

TWENTY-THREE

The Family

- Christmas 1900 -

The three little Watson girls were all dressed up, ready for Christmas dinner. They sat as still as they could in the parlor, waiting for their pa to come in from taking care of the animals. Ma was still in the kitchen with Aunt Beatrice, putting the food on the table for dinner.

Ma had shooed them out of the kitchen after Mamie dropped the cream pitcher and Irene stepped in it and tracked it all over the floor. She sent them to wait for Pa in the "Christmas room" and Laura was tasked with watching the two younger ones, making sure they did not get into any of the gifts under the tree.

The parlor had finally been updated with some beautiful red upholstered chairs, a gorgeous dark blue loveseat and a new rag rug. Belle had sent away to Pennsylvania for several crystal "puffy" oil lamps, etched with a Cherub face design. Joel often wondered if she ordered those in honor of little LeRoy, who was an angel now.

It was a very pleasant room. They called it the "Christmas room" during this time of year because that was where the Christmas tree and gifts were kept. Pine boughs with holly berries and other decorations festooned the windows.

Laura had turned eight years old that year, Irene was six, and Mamie was almost four. Irene had been named for Belle's aunt and Mamie's name was actually Mary, after Belle's mother. Irene couldn't say "Mary" when she was little. Instead, she called her Mamie, and the name stuck.

The three girls played well together, for the most part. The family was lucky to have Mrs. Ware's help as Belle was pregnant again. Belle had not been feeling well during this pregnancy. She had a few months to go. They were hoping for a boy this time.

Joel finally came in the door. The girls ran to him and jumped on him—Laura on his back, Irene in his arms and Mamie holding onto his leg.

"Can we open presents now? Can you light the candles on the tree now? Can I have my Christmas candy now?"

Joel laughed. "No, Mamie, we will wait and open presents after dinner. Irene, we'll light the candles then too. And no, Laura, of course you cannot eat candy right before dinner. What would your mother say?"

The girls giggled, and soon Belle called them in for Christmas dinner. They had a Christmas ham, sweet potatoes, apple biscuits, creamed corn, and plum pudding. As always, Mrs. Ware had made her famous Gingerbread cookies before she left to spend Christmas with her sister.

The family sang Christmas carols that night as was their custom. It always made Belle think of her childhood Christmases—and of those happy times before they lost their parents and their darling LeRoy.

After the caroling, the family sat in the parlor and opened presents. Belle had made Laura and Irene new dresses along with matching dresses for their dolls. Mamie got her first real doll. Beatrice opened her mother's pearl ring, which Belle had promised to give her when she was eighteen. Belle had made Joel a beautiful new banded-collar striped shirt with a five-button pleated placket.

"It's so fine," Joel said to Belle. "I will wear it with pride to the New Year's dance this year. Now open your gift."

Belle opened the small box. Inside was a beautiful gold locket on a chain. It had a scripted B on the front. Inside were two locks of hair. Both locks had been procured by Mrs. Ware who had wisely foreseen a day when Belle would want a lock of both her mother's and son's hair, as was the custom.

"Oh, Joel," Belle said, her eyes shining with the beginning of tears "I will treasure this always."

Belle still grieved for LeRoy and for her mother, just like he did. Joel knew she would be comforted by wearing the locket. It was a physical link to those lost loved ones.

After all the presents were opened and the girls were tucked into bed, Joel and Belle blew out the candles, dampened the fire and made their way upstairs. In their bedroom. Joel took Belle's hands and asked her to undress for him. He sat on the bed to look at her.

"I want to see you in the candlelight," he whispered. Belle took off her clothes slowly, until she needed help with her corset. Joel got up and helped to untie the corset. He began caressing her breasts and her pregnant belly. Then he picked her up and carried her to bed. He entered her slowly, savoring every moment until they both climaxed.

After, as they lay in each other's arms, Joel expressed his worry over her tiredness.

"Mildred said it is normal to feel this way with a fifth pregnancy. And I'm older than I was four years ago when I had Mamie," Belle said. "Of course I am tired. But Mrs. Ware is very helpful. She'll be back from her sister's house tomorrow, and I promise to take it easier."

Joel caressed her belly. "I am happy about the new baby, but you are so precious to us. Perhaps this one should be our last."

"Impossible!" she said, kissing him. "We could never give this up." And to prove the point, she kissed him until they made love again.

As they were falling asleep, Joel said sleepily, "You're right, Belle. Neither one of us could ever give this up."

. . .

The next two months went by slowly for Belle. The pregnancy just did not feel right. Her ankles were swollen, and she was exhausted all the time. She felt dizzy at times and had headaches.

Doctor Gordon started to come see her every week. Belle and Joel could tell he was concerned.

Finally, when Belle had only five weeks to go, the doctor took Joel aside. "Belle's blood pressure has increased slowly over the past weeks.

I'm starting to worry that your wife may have preeclampsia," the doctor confided. "We don't know what causes it. Unfortunately, it is a very serious condition."

"What happens to her and the baby if she has it?"

"They could both die. It is very dangerous. I'm sorry to say we don't have a cure. She should probably have the baby sooner rather than later, as some mothers have survived by having their baby early. I can do a procedure called amniotomy that might bring on labor. But it doesn't always work, and they could both die if it doesn't. Not to mention, being born too early could be fatal to the baby," he said, shaking his head.

"Let's bring on the labor," Joel said. "We can't lose Belle."

"We would have to get your wife's permission for that," Dr. Gordon said.

But Belle refused to put her child in danger. "I already lost one child." she said firmly. "I won't lose another if I can help it."

"But my darling, you could easily die if you don't try this," Joel begged. "Think of me—think of the girls—and Beatrice! We can't do without you."

"You most certainly will die if we don't intervene," said Doctor Gordon. "The baby could live, but you won't."

"But the baby has a better chance if I go full term?"

"If you make it that long! Belle, you need to do this. Your family needs you," Doctor Gordon said sternly.

"What will you do to me if I say yes?"

"I will perform an amniotomy, which means I will break your waters. This will put you into labor. I feel it is your only chance," the doctor replied.

"Can we wait until tomorrow?" Belle asked. "I'm not quite ready for the baby yet. And I want to spend some time with the girls."

"Of course," replied the doctor. "I will come back at noon tomorrow. Please be sure the midwife and Mrs. Fraser are here," he said to Joel.

After the doctor left the room, Belle asked Joel to leave the room and check on the girls so she could get some sleep. In reality, she knew she was about to break down, and she was afraid of upsetting Joel any further.

Lying in her bed, she covered her mouth and sobbed and sobbed. This was so unfair. She had three little girls and a new baby to raise, and Beatrice still needed her too.

How would Joel survive? They were dependent on each other for everything. They were each other's whole world. He would be all alone, raising their three girls and a new baby too. How would he manage that? How could he cope?

She would not see her girls grow up, she realized. Would she even get to hold her new baby in her arms? A fresh burst of grief hit her.

She felt a sudden, sharp pain in her head. She cried out, clutching her head.

By the time Joel reached their room, Belle was gone.

The doctor had not left yet. He ran upstairs, took Belle's pulse, and pronounced Belle dead.

"Her blood pressure rose and she had a fatal stroke," he said sadly. "There is nothing we could have done. I'm so sorry, Joel. But let's see if we can save the baby."

The doctor performed a cesarean operation to save the baby. But the little boy whom they had decided to name Howard after Joel's grandfather, was born too early and only lived a few hours.

Beatrice and the girls held little Howie before he had breathed his last. The girls could not seem to understand why he didn't cry and what had happened to their mother, especially Mamie.

"But when will she wake up?" Mamie asked when Joel brought her in to kiss her mother goodbye.

"We will see her in heaven again someday," Joel answered. "But she is gone from this earth now, little one."

As the girls looked at their mother, they seemed confused.

"But who will take care of us now?" Laura asked Joel.

"Mama will when she gets back from heaven, right Pa?" Irene answered.

Joel couldn't think of what to say. Beatrice dried her eyes and brought the girls downstairs. She sat the three little girls down in the parlor.

"Your ma is gone but your pa and I will take care of you, Mrs. Ware too," Beatrice told them. "We all need to look after each other like your ma would expect us to. We will all miss her but we will be ok, I promise."

The girls looked at her incomprehensibly. It would take time for them to understand.

Grief and anguish blurred the next two days. The Frasers came over to take care of them all—Joel, Beatrice, and the girls. They would bury Belle and Howie next to LeRoy when the ground thawed in the spring. Having them buried with LeRoy was a comfort to Joel. At least they would be together forever.

Three days later, they had a memorial service at the church. It was heartbreaking to see the two coffins side by side. Looking at the child sized coffin brought back those terrible feelings of grief for LeRoy as well. Joel tried to stay strong for the girls but broke down and cried during the service.

Laura and Irene both sobbed during the service. Beatrice held them close to her. trying not to break down. They were old enough so that they were beginning to understand. Mamie cried too, but mostly because everyone else was. Her pa picked her up and held her.

But she still didn't really comprehend that her mother wasn't coming back.

The next few months were tough ones on Joel and the girls. Mamie kept asking for her mother. One day Laura lost her temper with her.

"Stop asking that—don't you understand? She's never coming back!" she shouted.

Mamie pushed Laura with all her might and screamed at her. "You hush up! She is so coming back!"

Mrs. Ware had to pull them apart. Irene just sat in the corner, crying.

Pa made Laura apologize to Mamie. Things calmed down and Mamie stopped asking for her mother. In some ways, that made them all feel even sadder.

Beatrice walked around with red eyes, trying not to cry in front of the girls. Mrs. Ware was even quieter than usual. Even George and Zeke moped around. Joel and Belle's happy home seemed like a thing of the past, never to return. Belle had been the heart of their lives and without her, there was no joy.

The girls all had nightmares for weeks. Joel grieved for his son Howie as well. He wondered—how could their loving home have turned into such a place of misery? He knew Belle would have wanted them to stop grieving and get on with life. But he just couldn't seem to do it. He walked around hollow-eyed, trying to be both mother and father to the girls, and feeling like he failed them every day. On top of that, he was ever so lonely.

Nights were the worst. He would lie in bed, aching for his dear wife, longing for her touch. How could he go on without her?

But he did. The next day would come, and he went on.

Three months later, Belle's cousin Missy arrived with her two children—Ezzie, who was nine, and Willy who was eight. They all stayed in the big house, kids doubling up in rooms.

Billy, Missy's husband and Joel's stepbrother, had died a few months before of scarlet fever. Missy's parents had traveled to Montana and had just brought them back to Tethertown to live.

Missy and her mother decided that she should go stay at Joel's to help with the girls and to help pull them all out of their misery. They could see that it was too much for him in his state of grief, even with Beatrice's and Mrs. Ware's help. They hoped that Missy and Joel could support each other. Both of them were grieving.

It was a bit of a scandal in town that they were both living in the same house, but Missy's parents paid no attention to the gossip. They spent as much time as they could out at the farm as well, helping out and taking care of the children.

It was the best decision they could have made. After just a few days, the five children began to play together happily. They laughed and smiled again. They went on adventures, swam in the pond, chased the chickens, and of course got into many arguments, especially Laura and Willy.

Missy and Joel were a comfort to each other as well. They often talked about Billy and Belle, sometimes crying, but also laughing and reminiscing about their respective courtships.

One August night after everyone was in bed, Missy went downstairs for a glass of water and found Joel on the porch, looking very sad. Without even thinking about it, she came over to embrace him. They began kissing.

At that moment, Joel realized how hungry he had been for Belle's touch. But Belle was gone. Missy was here, willing in his arms. Without even thinking, he led her to his bedroom and they made love silently.

"Are you alright?" Joel asked her afterwards. "I didn't mean for that to happen."

"Neither did I," Missy replied. "But I think we both needed that. However, this must not happen again."

"It's time for you to go back to town, then," Joel said sadly.

"The children need to go to school starting in two weeks anyway. Should Laura and Irene come to town and live with us during the school week?" she asked.

"Oh no, I will drive them each morning," Joel replied. "Mamie and I could not do without them. Not yet, anyway."

"I wonder if you should get a place in town," Missy said. "Just to stay in for a few days a week so you don't have to make that long trip every day. It could be a fresh start. Zeke and George are doing a good job running this place, aren't they? And I'm sure Mrs. Ware wouldn't mind being in town, and it would be good for the girls to have friends around more. Mamie could play with the Smith girl in town, who is her age. She will be lonely without her sisters."

Joel sighed. "Beatrice would probably love to be in town as well. Belle and I had talked about that," he said. "Belle had her eye on old man White's house, which is still for sale. I bet I could get it at a decent price. It's nice and big, and that could work."

"Our children could spend more time together," Missy said. "They have become close this summer, especially Ezzie and Irene, despite their three-year age difference."

"And Laura and Willy, although they fight a lot." Joel said. "I would love to spend more time with you as well. You have been such a comfort to me. But I don't intend to ever remarry. I had a stepfather, and I would not inflict a stepmother on my girls."

"Not even me?" Missy asked sadly. "I love them already as my own."

"Well, maybe someday," Joel said slowly. "But neither of us is ready for that yet."

"No, we aren't." Missy answered. "Well, think about it anyway. Goodnight Joel." She got up to dress and quietly went back to the room she was sharing with Beatrice.

TWENTY-FOUR

Beatrice

Beatrice looked out the kitchen window at the beautiful September day and sighed. Belle had been gone about six months, and it seemed impossible that she would never see her dear sister again. She felt her absence every day. Her heart was heavy, and she was lonely.

Beatrice had been keeping busy with taking care of the girls, especially since Missy left. Mrs. Ware did the household work and cooking, but someone had to keep an eye on those three, especially Laura, who was always getting into something she shouldn't.

Why, just yesterday she was with them outside, about to go into town to register Laura and Irene for school. She had dressed the girls up in their Sunday best to make a good impression. She went inside for only five minutes, and when she returned all three girls had found a big puddle and were stomping around in the mud, ruining their good clothes. She was mighty upset with them—that was a lot of work, doing all the laundry— not to mention they all had to change clothes. But Joel refused to punish them.

"You're too soft on them," Beatrice said to him. "Belle would have tanned their behinds for making all that extra work for Mrs. Ware. How are they going to learn if we don't discipline them?"

"I just can't bear to make them any more unhappy than they are," he said. "Poor little girls."

"Poor little girls, my foot!" Beatrice said vehemently. "They are taking advantage of your good nature. Remember, Joel, I lost my Ma too at the age of ten, but you and Belle still kept me in line. It's good for them."

"You're right, of course," he admitted.

But Joel just never could be strict with the girls. That was up to Beatrice.

For the most part, when school was in session, life was easier. The only problem was the 45-minute trip to and from town every day. Most of the time, Joel took Laura and Irene himself. But when the weather turned cold, it was more difficult.

One night at dinner, Joel announced that he had bought a house in town. "It's large and I think we will move there for part of the year, especially when school is in session," he said.

"Which house is it?" Beatrice asked curiously.

"It's old man White's house," he replied.

"Oooh, Joel! That is a beautiful place." Beatrice said agog.

The seller told Joel that the house had been built by Robert White who was a rich banker in the late 1880s. He had commissioned a New York architect to come and build his house in the Second French Revival style. Joel didn't really care about all of that, he just wanted a home with plenty of room for his girls. However, he had to admit that it was a pretty impressive house. The wooden-shingled light gray house had a two pitched roof with big dormers and black patterned shingles. There were deep eaves with decorative brackets. He knew the girls would like it. It had been on the market for a while and had been priced too high, in his opinion. Joel was able to negotiate the price down and thought he got a pretty good deal on it.

If only Belle could have lived there too. She would have loved it.

Everyone was excited, especially Beatrice. Maybe she could have a social life again! She had missed her friends and all the events they had—picnics, dances, dinners at each other's houses. She was thrilled.

"May I have my own room?" Laura asked. "Irene and Mamie are always getting into my things. I need privacy. After all, I am nine years old now."

"Well, it has five bedrooms, so I think you are in luck," Pa answered. "Mrs. Ware will have a very nice bedroom on the first floor and the other four bedrooms are upstairs. They aren't very big rooms, but they will do. So, I suppose Irene and Mamie can share, and you can have your own room as the oldest, Laura."

Irene complained, but Mamie was quiet. She liked sharing a room with her sisters.

"When can we move in?" asked Beatrice. "And will we still come out here in the summer?"

"Oh yes, and I imagine Missy and your cousins will too," Joel replied. "I want to paint and fix a few things before we move in. Plus, I need to get some furniture and beds. Maybe you can help me with that, Beatrice? If you can, I think we could manage to move in by next month."

"I would be happy to," Beatrice said with a big smile on her face.

Soon, the family moved into the "Town House," as they called it. The farm was still home, of course, but it was nice to be in town. The girls could play with friends, and Beatrice had a social life again. It was good for Joel to have a change of scenery, too. He needed to let go and move forward. He hoped that being away from the farm where his two sons and beloved wife had died would help him to do so, although he still had to spend several days out there every week. There was always so much to do. He decided he would eventually have to hire a foreman for the farm if he wanted to spend more time with his daughters in town.

One evening after they moved in, Beatrice and Laura sat together in the parlor to work on their needlepoint. Laura was still learning and needed lots of help. As they worked together, Beatrice talked about how Belle had taught her to needlepoint.

"She was so patient with me. I never had her talent with the needle, but she continued to encourage me anyway," she said.

Laura put her needlepoint down and looked at Beatrice sadly.

"I'm starting to forget what her face looked like. Even when I look at her photograph, she doesn't seem real."

"I know. It's part of life, I guess. I can't remember my mother's face either. But we can remember who they were. We need to talk about her more, especially with your sisters. They will lose all of their memories of your ma if we don't try."

"Tell me a story about her," Laura asked.

Beatrice closed her eyes and a memory came to her. One she hadn't thought of for many years.

"Your ma was always a good big sister but she did like to tease me when we were children. One day, her friend Sophie had come over to play, something your ma had been looking forward to for a long time. Our mother asked me to leave them alone to play, but I wanted to be with them so badly. Finally, Mother said I could help them make ice cream as a special treat but then I had to leave them alone. We all took turns crank-ing the ice cream bucket—it seemed like it took forever—then finally it was ready and we each got a bowl of ice cream. Your ma then proposed a contest—whoever could take the biggest bite of ice cream would win. I wanted to prove that I could be one of the "big girls" so I shoved a huge bite of ice cream into my mouth. Of course, it gave me a brain freeze and then a headache. At first they both laughed but then your ma felt bad. She spent the rest of the afternoon rubbing my temples and taking care of me even though her friend was there. And I let her even though it didn't hurt anymore, and pretty much ruined her visit with Sophie. But she never said anything."

Beatrice paused, remembering. "That was your ma—always one to take care of others, to put others first. She was a born mother. Later, after our mother died, she was a loving mother to me, even through all of her grief. She was a pretty special lady."

Laura began to cry. "I miss her," she said.

Beatrice blinked back tears and then moved to sit next to Laura. She hugged her while she cried in her arms.

"Thank you for reminding me of that story," Beatrice said after a while. "I think I will share it with everyone tonight at dinner. I think your pa would like to hear it too, don't you?"

Laura sniffed and nodded her head. Then the two dried their tears and picked up their needlepoint again.

TWENTY-FIVE

Joel

By the end of October, the Watsons had settled nicely into their house in Tethertown. Joel could see that all the girls were happier. Beatrice had friends to gossip with and dances to go to, the girls all had their school friends, and Mamie played with Winifred Smith almost every day. Even Mrs. Ware was happier, now that she could just pop over to the general store any time.

Joel was the lost one.

He spent most days out at the farm and returned to town by sunset. The trip by horse and wagon was about an hour each way, but Joel didn't mind. On the way back to Tethertown, he would use the time to think about what he had accomplished that day and plan for the next day. In the early mornings he would sometimes talk to Belle. Out on the lonely road with the sun coming up he felt closer to her, as if she were at the farm waiting for him.

More times than not, at least one of the girls was over at Missy's parents' house playing when he returned home. He often stopped there on his way back home and would have tea with Missy and her parents. Missy and Joel remained a great source of support for each other.

He still dreamed of Belle. He would wake up, aroused, and reach for her. But she was gone.

Then one night, it was Missy he dreamed of. After that, he started dreaming of Missy and longed for her almost every night. Finally, while sitting with her on his front porch one day, he blurted out, "I wonder if you would ever consider returning to my bed sometime."

Missy looked at him shocked, then smiled.

"I would love nothing better. But Joel, I could become pregnant. I dare not take the risk," she said.

"I understand," he said shamefacedly. "I'm sorry to be so forward in asking such a question. But I do think of you and our night together fairly often,"

"As do I," she said softly. "But how can we take that chance?"

Joel knelt at her feet. "If we were engaged, would you consider it?"

Missy looked at him, surprised. "I thought you said that you would never remarry. Have you changed your mind?"

"Not yet," he said quickly. "But if you became pregnant, I would marry you right away, of course. If not, we could just remain engaged. What do you think?"

"Joel, at some point I may want a new life with a husband and home," Missy said sharply. "If we become engaged, I would expect to marry at some point, even if not right away."

Joel was silent for a while. "Give me some time," he said at last. "We'll set a date for next August. How about the anniversary of our coming together for the first time? By then I will know whether I can feel right about marrying again. But I long for us to be together, dear Missy. I can't sleep at night for thinking of you."

"And if I become pregnant?" she asked again.

"We will marry immediately, I promise. I will be happy to do so because that will show me that it was meant to be." he answered.

Joel went to St. Joseph the next week and bought Missy a simple diamond ring. He stayed in town on Saturday night, gave Mrs. Ware the night off, sent the girls and Beatrice to their friends' house, and invited Missy to dinner.

After they ate Mrs. Ware's fried chicken, Joel gave Missy the ring. "I hope to marry you someday," he said, looking into her eyes. "But in the meantime…"

Missy did not say a word, but let him put the ring on her finger and then took his hand and led him upstairs. She stood in his room and Joel began undressing her slowly, savoring each moment, kissing her all over. They fell into bed and began to explore each other's bodies.

Joel had been afraid that he would not be able to keep himself from comparing Missy to Belle, but that was not the case. Missy was so very different from Belle. She was an insatiable lover, knew what she wanted, and she let Joel know. Belle had been shyer in that regard. Missy was also able to excite him in a new way, a way he had not felt before. The passion they had with each other was surprising to both of them. When they finished, they were both spent.

After a while, Missy got up and began to get dressed.

"Don't leave," Joel said softly. "Let me hold you just a little longer."

"No, I must go. I don't want my parents to wonder where I am so late. But if you are a good boy, I will be back soon." She smiled wickedly at him.

"Tomorrow night?" he asked hopefully.

"We have two houses with pretty observant children and my parents, not to mention Beatrice and Mrs. Ware. We have to be careful," she said seriously. "I need to be able to hold my head up high in this town."

Joel groaned.

"We'll figure something out," she answered. "We may need to find a secret hideaway to meet."

Joel perked up. "Well, my Uncle Don is out of town for the next few months. I am keeping an eye on his house."

"Perfect," Missy smiled. "We will just need to sneak out like Romeo and Juliet once in a while. Now I need to go. I think I will walk home and cool off a bit. I am sure I look a bit flushed."

Joel grinned at her. "Yes, you do. Shall I walk you home? And should we meet tomorrow at Uncle Don's?"

"We will see," she answered. "But I will walk alone tonight. Now, goodnight, dear fiancé. You will need to come to dinner tomorrow so we can tell our children and my parents about our engagement. Could you bring the ring then?"

"Yes, I will," he answered.

Missy took off the ring, kissed him, and left the room.

Joel sighed and went to sleep quickly. He slept better than he had since Belle died.

TWENTY-SIX

The affair with Joel was the most exciting thing Missy had ever experienced. They would leave notes for each other in the old oak tree in Joel's yard, setting up when they could meet. Some nights she literally snuck out of her parents' house like a teenager. Joel was a man so he did not have to sneak—he just walked out the door, and no one would ever question him. Mrs. Ware stayed at the house, so he never had to worry about leaving the girls alone.

They would meet in the guest bedroom in Uncle Don's house. In that room, they both experienced lovemaking like they never had before. It got to the point that Missy was thinking about being in that room with Joel almost every day. She began to think something was wrong with her. Did other women feel this way? She never heard of any who did. But it really wasn't something any lady would discuss. So, she did not know.

Luckily, she had not become pregnant—yet. She wondered if she could possibly be past that worry—she was thirty-eight now—or if it was just a matter of time.

One morning, after a particularly late night with Joel, her mother asked casually, "So how are you and Joel getting along?"

The way she said it, Missy could tell that she knew. She blushed crimson.

"We are fine," she answered warily.

"I hope you are being careful. You know there are certain times of the month where you are more likely to get pregnant," Irene Hughes said.

"Yes, I know about that," she mumbled.

"Good. But of course, no time is completely safe." Her mother got up and left the room.

As much as she enjoyed her time with Joel, Missy was also enjoying her independence. She was not sure she wanted to give that up and be anyone's wife again.

Supposedly, they were to wed in about six months' time. Well, she would play it by ear. Perhaps they'd just keep going as they were, and marry if they had to.

Luckily, Joel's Uncle Don had decided to spend another year away, so they continued to use his house for their late-night trysts.

One night as they lay together in Don's house, Missy shared her thoughts about her independence.

Joel listened and thought a while. "Let's just stay engaged and see what happens," he responded. "I do love the excitement of our secret meetings. Let's not give those up." He leaned on one arm, smiling wickedly at her.

"Oh no, let's not stop," she said. "But my mother has figured out what we're doing. I just hope Pa doesn't."

"Well, if he does, we will have to get married right away," he said. "Or we will have to break it off."

"Let's not worry about that tonight," she murmured and began kissing him again.

. . .

June came and Missy, Joel, and all the children moved back to the farm. Her parents rode out to the farm most days. People in town seemed to accept the situation better as they were engaged, but friends began to ask her about wedding plans.

Nights in Joel's room were exciting and dangerous. They both worried that Ezzie, at least, would figure it out. Beatrice still spent most of her time in town, but when she was at the farm, they had to be even more careful.

Missy tried to be evasive, but she could see her father and others were beginning to get suspicious. As much as she loved being on the farm with

Joel all summer—especially the nights—she still was not sure she wanted to marry right now.

Joel left it up to her. He was very happy with their arrangement. However, Missy was sure that it was only a matter of time until her father caught her, so she decided to rent a three-bedroom house in town for herself and her two children. It was getting a bit cramped at her parents' house anyway, and Willy was tired of sharing a room with his sister. Missy was starting to long for her own place. Her plan was to move in after the summer.

The problem with her plan was money. Missy had no source of income. Her parents supported her while she lived at their house, but if she moved, how would she pay for food and rent?

Joel was happy to pay for the rent when she told him of her plan, but she did not like that idea. What if he changed his mind about her or met someone else? She couldn't take that risk.

Sadly, her problem was solved in July. Her father died of a sudden heart attack. After the funeral, she and her mother met with his attorney. It turned out that her father had quite a large amount of money, left to him by his parents. In his will, he left half of the money to Missy's mother, and the other half to Missy.

Even though she now had the financial means, Missy couldn't leave her mother alone. She saved the money and decided to wait for a few months. But she was determined to eventually move out. She wanted her own place so that Ezzie and Willy could have their own rooms.

August came and went. The wedding was postponed. Her father's death was the excuse they gave, but really, neither of them was ready for marriage. So they continued their clandestine love affair. No one seemed the wiser.

That was, except for Beatrice. She was on a buggy ride one fall evening with one of her beaus and saw Missy walking to Don's house late at night. She didn't think Missy saw her, but she told Joel the next day what she'd seen.

Joel looked at Beatrice and realized he would need to be honest with her. Beatrice was twenty-one and could handle the truth.

Her reaction surprised him.

"Well, I already suspected that something was going on. I am happy for you both," she said. "I don't think either of you seems ready to get married right now, but I am glad you have found some happiness in your own way."

"Thank you for understanding," he said quietly. "This does not take anything away from the way I felt—and still feel—about Belle. But I was so lonely and miserable before. I feel much happier now."

"That's good. And I am sure Belle would want you to be happy. She would never want you to be miserable," Beatrice said.

"Yes, I believe you are right," Joel said. "I feel sure that she would understand."

TWENTY-SEVEN

Walter

-1910-

Standing in the green pasture on his family's farm, Walter felt a black cloud descending on him. This was the day they would leave their farm, the only home he had ever known. The thought made him sick to his stomach.

The Bauers had come relocated to the United States from Germany before Walter was born. His brothers had been born in Bavaria. His parents, Garman and Sophia, emigrated because they did not believe Germany was a safe place to live with Kaiser Wilhelm in charge. They thought the Kaiser was a bloodthirsty tyrant.

Garman's Uncle Franz had immigrated to America in 1873 and had purchased land in Kentucky, where he now had a cattle farm. Franz was getting older, so welcomed Garman's help. In the year 1897, the family sailed to New Orleans and made their way by train with the little money they had left to Kentucky. Walter was born shortly after they arrived at the farm.

Walter had a wonderful childhood growing up on the farm with his two older brothers Friedrich and Hans. They all loved to be outdoors, playing in the meadow and in the barn. They did chores and helped their father on the farm when they got home from school. In the winter they would have snowball fights and would swim in the pond when the summer came. Their childhoods consisted of hard work on the farm, followed by play. It was a happy childhood.

But Uncle Franz died when Walter was ten years old. Walter's father inherited the farm, so they continued to work and live there. Times were hard. Bad weather, cattle disease, and higher feed prices forced the Bauers to sell off some of their land.

Just as the market started to rebound, disaster struck. It was a sunny morning in May and Garman did not feel well. Still, he got himself out of bed and made his way out to the fields to check on the livestock.

When Garman did not show up for breakfast, Friedrich rode out to the field to check on him. There he found his father, lying on the ground. Friedrich could not rouse him. He held his fingers on his father's neck to feel for a pulse, but there was nothing. His father was gone.

Sophia was devastated, but true to her upbringing, she stayed strong for her sons. Not a tear was shed.

After they buried Garman, Sophia and Fredrich met with the banker in town. He had reluctantly lent money to Garman the year before to buy more cattle. A large payment of $400 was overdue. The Bauers had no money in the bank to pay it.

"You will have to sell the farm, " the banker told them. "Only then will you have the money to repay this debt. Garman knew this, but he was putting it off, hoping for a miracle."

"He is with the Lord now," Sophia said sorrowfully in her native German. "His miracle was to go to heaven. We will sell."

Soon after, Sophia wrote to her Aunt Gerta in Missouri, who had invited them to stay many times. She was getting older, and needed someone to help her. The family would move to Tethertown, Missouri and move in Aunt Gerta's house.

That last morning, Walter walked out to the fields on his father's farm. Looking around, his eyes welled up. He loved this place. Leaving this land felt like losing his father all over again. He had hoped to raise cattle with his father and brothers here. It had been their own little piece of paradise- their home. But it was not to be.

With some of the money left over from the sale of the farm, the Bauers bought train tickets. They arrived in St. Joseph, Missouri in June where they were met at the station by Aunt Gerta's hired hand. The family moved into Aunt Gerta's home in Tethertown.

After just a few days, Hans and Friedrich promptly got jobs as cow-hands out of town. They were grown men and were ready to be independent, now that their family farm was gone. Walter decided to stay in town with his mother and find a job there.

Soon he was working at the lumber yard. It wasn't a bad job, but he missed his home, his brothers, and his father. He especially longed for the life he had on the farm—being outside in all sorts of weather, working with the livestock, and the feeling of working in a place that belonged to his family.

I'll never have that again, he thought sadly.

Still, there were good things about being in town. His mother was able to find other German immigrant women and joined a quilting circle. She enjoyed taking care of their Aunt Gerta. She was happy to have Walter close by.

They began attending church, although he was not sure his mother could understand everything the preacher was saying. Through the church he began to hear of various activities for people his age.

He overheard a beautiful girl talking about an Ice Cream Social in the park for young people the following week. His mother noticed how Walter looked at her, and later that day encouraged him to go.

Walter was shy. He always felt tongue-tied around strangers, especially girls. But he knew his mother was right and made himself go to the Ice Cream Social.

As he entered the park he ran into his new friend Carl Reade, a young lawyer who had also just moved to town. Walking around with Carl, Walter saw that same beautiful girl from church, laughing with a group of friends. He couldn't take his eyes off her.

She was tall, with creamy white skin and gorgeous auburn hair under an elaborately festooned straw hat. Even from across the park, he could see she had beautiful big blue eyes and a full mouth with luscious red lips. She took his breath away.

"Who is that?" he asked Carl.

"That's Laura Watson," Carl replied. "Her father is a well-off cattle farmer and has a house in town as well as a big farm. She's so pretty that lots of fellas have been wanting to court her, but she won't have any of them. I guess she's picky. And, as a matter of fact, I'm thinking of courtin' her sister Irene. Do you want me to introduce you?"

"No, no, that's all right," Walter replied nervously. He had not dressed up as nicely as some of the other young men, and felt a bit embarrassed. He knew that first impressions were important.

Carl shrugged. "Suit yourself," he said.

Walter would need to think of a way to meet her. And he would need to have his mother make him some new clothes.

It's probably hopeless, he thought glumly. *I don't have much to offer a girl like that. But I gotta try.*

TWENTY-EIGHT

Laura

Laura walked home from school for the last time on the cold, December day. Her birthday was the next day. She would be eighteen years old. Her pa had promised she could be finished with school and start her adult life when she turned eighteen.

Her girlfriends Bessie and Susannah were giving her a surprise birthday party at the Grange the next evening. Well, it was supposed to be a surprise, but almost fourteen-year-old Mamie had let it slip the day before. Only Laura had overheard her, and they decided that Laura should pretend to be surprised.

As she walked in the cold, Laura wondered who would be invited. There were all the fellow students she had gone to school with over the years, and there were some other people her age that had moved into town as well.

One person she had noticed in particular was Walter Bauer. He lived in town with his mother and worked in the lumber yard. They had moved here from Kentucky. She had heard that his father had died and they wanted a fresh start. Walter had a maiden aunt in Tethertown who invited them to stay.

Laura had seen Walter in church and admired his seriousness. Some of the boys her age—supposedly men now—still acted immaturely. She was not sure how old Walter was, but he was no immature boy. He was a man and oh, so handsome! It made her heartbeat faster just to look at him.

Bessie had teased her about Walter when she noticed Laura watching him in church.

"All the girls are swooning over him, especially Addie Osbourne. She has set her cap for him." Bessie confided. "But did you know he is only twenty? I would have thought he was older. He seems so mature."

"Have you spoken to him?" Laura had asked. "I would like to meet him. He seems so mysterious and interesting, unlike the other boys in this town."

"No, not yet," Bessie answered. "You might have to go introduce yourself to him."

"Oh, I don't know, that seems so forward," Laura said doubtfully. "My Aunt Irene would have a fit if she saw me doing that."

"Well, don't let her see you then!" Bessie said, smirking. "But you better hurry before Addie gets her hooks into him."

Laura, Bessie, and Susannah had never liked Addie. Addie had been mean to Laura in school and was nasty to Laura's little sisters as well. She was constantly looking down on them, making catty remarks about their homemade dresses. All her dresses were store-bought as her father, a widower like Pa, gave her anything she wanted from the general store, which he owned. She also demanded he let her order dresses from a fancy dressmaker in St Joseph. She always had the most fashionable clothes.

Hurrying into the house, Laura threw off her coat, took off her hat, and headed towards the kitchen.

As Laura walked into the kitchen, Mrs. Ware looked up and asked, "Where are your sisters?"

"Irene is at Ezzie's house and Mamie is at Sally's house. Mrs. Ware. I'm through with school! Where's Pa?"

"Congratulations, Laura. Your pa went out to the farm, some problem with one of the pigs or something. By the way, we are having a big family dinner tonight to celebrate your birthday. Just in case you are busy with your friends tomorrow night," she said slyly.

"Who is coming?"

"Oh, your sisters, Beatrice, your pa, your Aunt Missy, Aunt Irene, Willy and Ezzie, I imagine. I'm making your favorite chocolate cake. Now shoo so I can concentrate!"

Laura went upstairs to take off her corset and relax. Lying on her bed, she wondered if Walter would be at her party. She hoped so. She really wanted to meet him. She closed her eyes and dreamed of dancing with the handsome Walter Bauer.

The thought made her sit up—would there even be music? Her pa had a gramophone and she and Bessie had some ragtime records, but she wondered if Bessie had even thought of that. She also doubted Walter would know how to dance to ragtime. Bessie, Susannah, and Laura had been practicing their ragtime dances—the Turkey Trot and the Texas Tommy. But she doubted any of the boys in town had.

Well, they could also play some waltzes, she supposed. Pa had some of those records. But she needed to make sure they brought the gramophone!

Mamie came bursting into her room. "What are you going to wear tomorrow night?" she whispered after closing the door. "I was going to wear my new blue silk. But is it too formal, do you think?"

"I can't answer you, as I know nothing about this party," Laura said. "You should ask Irene. What kind of party is it? Will they have dancing and music?"

"Oh yes, they are bringing over Pa's gramophone and all your records. So don't wear your tight yellow dress—you will want to dance. I know— you can wear your new dance dress Pa bought for you for your birthday in St. Jo. Irene picked it out. It's a ragtime dress, I think."

"Actually, I picked it out and told Irene. Please bring some of Pa's waltz records tomorrow also, will you?" Laura asked.

"I will. Probably some of the boys don't know how to waltz either, though," Mamie replied, rolling her eyes.

. . .

Laura's birthday dinner was lots of fun with her aunts and cousins. Willy kept teasing her about turning eighteen and looking for a husband.

"Oh no," Laura said. "I don't want to get married for many years. I want to have fun!"

Missy smiled at her. "What makes you think married life isn't fun?"

she asked.

"Well, as neither you nor Pa ever decided to remarry, I just assumed so." she answered.

The table went silent.

"Your Pa and I had our reasons," Missy said, glancing at Joel. "But I think we can both say we loved being married before."

"Oh yes," Pa said. "We both had very happy marriages. And I wish Belle and Billy were here to see how fine all of you have turned out. I did love being married to your ma, but decided to stay single after she died."

"So did I," Missy said, smiling at Joel. "We have each other's companionship when we want it, but also our independence. But I never regretted for a second being married to your Uncle Billy, Laura. Those were wonderful years."

Willy looked down at his plate and turned red. He had figured out the arrangement between his mom and Uncle Joel years ago.

Joel quickly changed the subject. "So, what will you do on your birthday, Laura? Do you have any plans?"

"Oh, yes. I will spend the night with Bessie at Susannah's house after we go into town for dinner at the cafe in town. It should be fun." Laura smiled.

"Well, now it's time for your birthday gift," her father announced.

Laura opened the gift—the dance dress—and acted surprised. "Thank you, Pa. I love it!" she declared, hugging him.

The dress was mauve with a large cream-colored plunging collar and split skirt for dancing. There was a silk ruffle (called a peplum) on the upper bodice that flared out below the high waistband. Below the bodice, an ankle-length split skirt tapered to a narrower base. It was like no dress any of them had worn before.

"Hey—isn't that a ragtime dance dress?" Ezzie asked.

Irene nudged her to be quiet in front of Joel. The girls were afraid he would not approve of ragtime dancing. Luckily, Joel did not seem to hear her.

The night of Laura's party turned out to be a beautiful crisp December evening. Susannah came by to walk Laura to dinner.

"Where's Bessie?" Laura asked.

"Oh, she's not feeling well," Susannah answered. "She said she would come over to my house later if she feels better. We'll just have dinner without her," she said nervously.

"Well, that's strange," Laura said. "I thought I saw her walk by my house earlier. My, you are certainly dressed up for dinner at the café."

Susannah eyed Laura suspiciously. "Is that your new dress from St Joseph? It is very modern with that hemline. It also is very festive for the café."

"Yes, I thought it would be fun to wear tonight. It was my birthday gift from Pa. It's a ragtime dance dress. I didn't tell Pa that as he might not approve. We can practice our ragtime dances at your house after dinner."

"Of course, say, is it OK if we stop by the Grange Hall? I promised to pick something up for my pa."

"What could he possibly have at the Grange Hall that you need to pick up? Look—there is Bobby Fallon walking into the building. I wonder what is going on," Laura said innocently.

"OK, so you figured it out. But act surprised!" Susannah begged. "Bessie tried so hard to make it a surprise."

"I will, don't worry," Laura laughed.

After acting completely shocked, Laura hugged her two friends and then looked around. Everyone she knew was there. The hall was decorated with streamers and a big burlap sign painted with "Happy Birthday Laura!" The gaslights were turned down low and a big table was piled high with food, along with a big bowl of punch.

Laura noticed her Aunt Missy sitting behind the punch bowl.

"Mrs. Ware and your aunts made most of the food," Bessie told her. "And I made the punch. We have to make sure none of the older boys put any moonshine in it. That is why your Aunt Missy is here. She is chaperoning and watching the punch."

"This is so nice. Thank you so much," Laura said, eyes shining. She hugged both Susannah and Bessie again.

She looked around and spotted Walter, standing on the side with one of her old school mates Addie chattering away at him. Addie had grown into a pretty young woman, with blonde ringlets and fair skin. Unfortunately, her personality did not reflect her sweet looks. She was still mean and nasty sometimes, just like when they were in school together—especially when it came to getting her own way. But even though Laura and her friends didn't like her, she had to be invited to the party. It would be the height of rudeness if she wasn't and reflect poorly on Laura.

"Bessie, can you introduce me to Walter? Were you the one who invited him?" Laura whispered to the girls.

"Actually, I did," Susannah said. "I saw him at the lumber yard when I went to go bring my pa his lunch and introduced myself. I told him about your birthday party. He seemed to know who you were. So, I invited him."

The girls walked up to Walter and said hello. Addie glared at them, but they ignored her.

Susannah introduced him to Bessie and Laura.

"So, this is your birthday party," Walter said. "Happy birthday, and thanks for inviting me."

"Well, I did not know about the party so I couldn't have invited you. But I'm glad you came," she said smiling shyly.

They heard a ragtime tune coming from the gramophone.

"Oh Walter, do you know how to dance to ragtime?" Addie asked him. "I love the Cakewalk and the Turkey Trot! Don't you?" Addie batted her eyelashes at him.

"No, can't say I do. Excuse me, ladies," Walter said, and walked away.

"Addie! You embarrassed him," Bessie said. "Just go find someone else to dance with and leave the poor man alone. C'mon Laura, let's go do the Turkey Trot." She grabbed Laura's hand and ran out on the floor.

Soon many of the partygoers were dancing to the ragtime tunes. After a while, Laura asked Bessie to put on a waltz. When she turned around, Walter was standing right next to her.

"I learned to waltz in Kentucky," he said. "Will you dance with me?"

"Of course," Laura said, smiling up at him.

Bessie was watching. As soon as the dance ended, she put on another waltz so they could keep dancing.

Laura was having a wonderful time. Not only was Walter handsome, but he was a good dancer. He was pretty quiet, though.

"Maybe you could teach me one of those ragtime dances sometime?" he said, looking down at her. "Perhaps I could come over to your house and you could show me? I want to be able to participate in all the fun here."

"I would be happy to," Laura said.

"Could I come over on Saturday? I only work a few hours then. Would you be at home at two o'clock?" he asked hopefully.

"Yes, I believe so. That is my pa's gramophone and my records, so I would be able to teach you with the music," she said. "But we should invite some of the other boys as well, as none of them seem to know the dances either."

Walter looked a little disappointed for a second, but then smiled. "That sounds fine," he said.

Another ragtime tune was put on and all the girls but Laura ran out on the dance floor.

"Thanks for dancing with me," Walter said. "I have to work early tomorrow, so I better go. I look forward to seeing you on Saturday."

"Yes," was all Laura could say.

As he walked away, he suddenly stopped and turned back around. "Happy birthday!" he said, grinning. Then he left.

"Well, thanks for runnin' him off," Addie said to Laura when she went to get some food. "He only danced with you and then he left. Honestly!" And she flounced off.

Laura, Bessie, and Susannah giggled.

Laura told her friends about her idea for a dance class at her house on Saturday.

"I'll see if I can get some of these boys to come," Bessie said. "We should invite some of the girls as well. But won't your parlor be too small?"

"Let's just invite a couple of boys and see how it goes," Laura suggested. "Then we can do it again, maybe here where there is more room."

"Well, I'm asking Marcus," Susannah said. "He's a good dancer."

"And you like him," Bessie said pointedly.

"Well, maybe," Susannah answered. "Who will you ask, Bessie?"

"I don't really have any romantic feelings for any of these boys, but I'll ask George. He likes to dance, and is so much fun."

"I suppose I will have to let Irene and Mamie come with Ezzie and Willy too," Laura sighed. "Ezzie will want to ask her latest beau, and Irene can just make do with Willy."

"It will be fun," Bessie said with a wink. "And you'll get to spend more time with Walter."

"Yes," Laura smiled.

. . .

In the end, the word got around so they had to move the dance lessons to the Grange Hall on Saturday. Most of the partygoers were coming. Laura and her friends were going to teach the Turkey Trot and the Texas Tommy, and Addie and her friend Melanie would teach the Cakewalk and the Foxtrot.

Laura needed to get word to Walter that they were going to meet at the Grange instead of her house, so the next day she screwed up her courage and walked over to the lumber yard. After looking around, she found Walter working alone in the back.

"Hello, Walter," she said.

Walter looked surprised, then pleased to see her. "Hello, Laura. How are you on this fine day?" he asked, smiling at her.

"I am well," she replied. "Thank you for coming to my party last night."

"I wish I could have stayed longer, but I had to be here before dawn. What time did the party end?"

"Oh, I don't know, maybe around ten-thirty? Anyway, I've come to tell you that your idea of dance lessons has caught on and now we are meeting at the Grange at two o'clock on Saturday. Lots of our friends are coming. I hope you are still coming?"

"Yes," he said. But he looked disappointed.

"But maybe you could come by my place a bit earlier and help me set up at the Grange?" she suggested.

"Hmm. I could get finished a bit early and come by at one o'clock. Would that work?" he asked.

"Yes, so, I will see you then?"

"See you then!" he answered, feeling a thrill go through him. She seemed to like him!

On Saturday, Walter came by the house promptly at 1:00. As soon as she heard the knock, Laura felt butterflies in her stomach. She composed herself and answered the door.

"Hello Laura," Walter said. He was trying not to stare, but she was so beautiful.

"Please come in. How are you today?" she asked nervously, taking his coat and hat.

"I am well. And how are you?"

"I am just fine. I thought we could sit in the parlor and have tea," Laura said.

"That sounds very nice," Walter answered.

"Of course, my pa wants to meet you. I hope you don't mind," she said anxiously. "He's a bit old-fashioned."

"Not at all. I would like to meet your father," Walter said, trying to smile.

What if her father doesn't think I'm good enough for her? Walter thought. *He probably won't—I'm just a poor boy working in a lumber yard with no prospects.*

Laura and Walter made their way to the elegant parlor where Joel was waiting. Laura introduced them and they shook hands.

Walter's fears of Laura's father looking down on him were unfounded. As it turned out, her pa and Walter had a lot in common. Walter had worked on a farm in Kentucky that had a few head of cattle. They had both struggled with the loss of their father. They both were passionate about farming. The two men discussed the latest theories on cattle feeding and disease prevention. Joel talked about the Model T he had his eye on in Kansas City. He was planning on purchasing it the following week and the two discussed how to drive and maintain an automobile. Walter said his boss at the lumber yard had one and said that a man had to be pretty skilled at changing tires to drive a Model T. Joel was impressed—Walter seemed to know a lot about farming—and automobiles.

"I've always been interested in them," Walter said. "I hope one day to be able to buy one of those Ford automobiles myself."

After a while, Laura cleared her throat and gave her father a pointed look.

"Well, I better get going," Pa said, taking the hint and standing up. "You young folks have fun with your dance lessons."

"We will," Laura said.

Walter stood up and shook Joel's hand. "It was nice to meet you, sir."

Joel nodded and left the room. Laura went over to the tea set and poured both of them a cup. "Milk or sugar?" she asked Walter.

"No, thank you," he said.

They sipped their tea in silence for a moment.

"When should we head over to the Grange?" Walter asked.

"Pretty soon. I'll need you to carry the gramophone and I'll bring the records. But I don't think the Grange will be open until two o'clock. So, we should wait a few more minutes," Laura answered.

The couple chatted for a while. Laura told him about their farm. Walter talked about living in Kentucky, his father's death, and how much he missed his family's farm.

"We decided we all wanted a fresh start, especially my mother," he told her. "And of course, we lost our farm because of the many debts my pa had taken on during the hard times. Anyway, my mother was unhappy there without my father. Luckily, my Aunt Gerta wrote and begged us to come. Aunt Gerta lives in her parents' old home in town, and there is plenty of room for us all."

Walter caught his breath and realized he hadn't talked about himself to anyone in a long time. Something about Laura made him feel so at ease, in spite of her gorgeous façade.

Laura spoke about her mother's passing and how hard it was for her.

"I still miss her sometimes," she said. "But Pa always took good care of us. He even moved us to town so we also could get a fresh start. I guess we have that in common," she said softly.

As they walked to the Grange a few minutes later, Laura realized she was falling for Walter already. He was so different from the boys in town. On top of that, he was kind and he was a good listener. He seemed to really want to hear what she had to say.

At the Grange, everyone had a good time learning the dances. It was a great success. The girls got together and decided to start having ragtime dances at least once a month.

Walter walked Laura home after the dance practice, bringing the gramophone inside.

"I had a wonderful time. May I call on you again?" he asked her hopefully.

"I did too. And yes, you may call on me again," Laura said.

Walter took her hand and kissed it. Then he smiled at her ruefully.

"I guess I am kind of old fashioned, like your father. Men probably don't kiss ladies' hands like that anymore."

"Thank you," was all Laura could think to say, her heart racing. She felt something she had never felt before. She wished he would grab her and kiss her all over.

"Oh my," she whispered after she closed the door. Irene and Mamie, who had been hiding and trying to hear from the dining room, accosted her right away.

"Is he going to be your new beau now? I heard him ask if he could call on you again," Mamie said excitedly.

"We couldn't help but overhear. We didn't mean to eavesdrop," Irene said apologetically.

"Yes, you did," Laura said, shaking her head, laughing.

"He kissed your hand, oh, how romantic!" Mamie sighed.

"I hope he is going to be my beau. But we will see," Laura answered and she went upstairs to dream of a future with the object of her desire, Walter Bauer.

TWENTY-NINE

Laura

Walter began calling on Laura as often as he could, at least several times a week. Her father had finally bought that Model T automobile from Kansas City, and he allowed Walter to take Laura on short rides around town. Walter was the only one Joel trusted to drive it. Laura and Walter also went for walks in the park, even on cold winter days. They both craved time alone with each other.

The couple attended dances at the Grange and walked home from church together. Walter began staying for Sunday supper, along with his friend Carl, who was courting Irene.

Laura had never been so happy. One February evening after a long walk, Walter pulled her behind a large sycamore tree where they could not be seen. There he took her face in his hands and kissed her for the first time. As he continued to kiss her, Laura felt as if she were melting in his arms. She wanted more.

Finally, Walter came to his senses and pulled back. "I am falling in love with you," he whispered to her.

"I am falling in love with you too," she said hoarsely and kissed him again. After that, the couple could hardly wait to be alone. Laura knew they had to be careful—her reputation could be ruined if people found out that she was kissing a man. But she could not seem to make herself care. She just wanted to be in Walter's arms.

. . .

One afternoon a few weeks later, Pa came home early from the farm. Laura was inside helping Mrs. Ware with the never-ending laundry. Her sisters were still in school.

"Laura?" he called as he entered the house. Laura hurried to greet him.

"Pa? What are you doing back? I thought you were going to spend the week out at the farm?" she said.

Pa announced that Mrs. Casey, their cook and housekeeper out on the farm, was ill and was moving back to her sister's house.

"Laura, I need you to move out to the farm for a time. Beatrice is busy with her charity work and helping Mrs. Ware with the girls, so that leaves you to take over as cook for the farmhands, doing their laundry, and keeping up the farmhouse. I realize this is not what you had planned for this month, but I need you to stay out there until either Mrs. Casey returns or until we find a new housekeeper. I'm sorry to ask you, but I don't have a choice right now," he said apologetically.

Of course, there was nothing to be done. "That is fine, pa. I'm happy to help out. When would I need to go?"

"As soon as you can be ready," he answered.

Laura packed up her things and then quickly called Susannah, who now worked at the general store. Laura wanted to let her know where she was going and to ask her a favor. Unfortunately, Susannah wasn't working that day and Addie, who was filling in, answered the phone. Laura would just have to ask Addie.

"Addie, can you let everyone know I have to be out at the farm for a few weeks?" she asked. "I hope you can especially let Walter know. He was supposed to come over later this week, but I will be gone by then."

"Certainly, Laura," Addie answered in a chipper voice. "I will let everyone know; don't you worry. Have a good time."

"I'm going out there to replace our farm housekeeper who is sick for a while, so it isn't for fun. I hope to be back in town in a few weeks."

"Oh, I hope so too," Addie said in a smarmy, insincere voice. "We will all miss you. Say, isn't your old beau Johnny still working out at your pa's farm? That might make the work more fun."

"He was never my beau, Addie. Please just let everyone know. Thank you."

Laura hung up the phone, annoyed at Addie. Leave it to Addie to bring up Johnny.

Johnny had a crush on Laura when they were in school, but she never returned the feeling. In fact, he gave her the creeps. She had forgotten he worked out at the farm. His father was their foreman, so it made sense.

I'll just have to avoid him as much as possible, she thought.

In the meantime, she would write Walter a note and leave it for Irene to deliver to him. Her note promised him she would be back soon and that she hoped he would not forget her. She left it on Irene's dresser and her father drove her out to the farm.

Unfortunately, when Mrs. Ware brought up Irene's clean clothes to put away, she didn't notice the note and it was pushed into a drawer under her clothing. Irene never saw it.

Out at the farm, Laura got busy right away. There was a stack of laundry, a dirty kitchen, and eggs to be gathered. Pa helped her out by gathering the eggs and lifting the heavy laundry tub full of soapy water into the mudroom so she could soak some of the dirty farmhands clothes. But then he had to hurry out to the barn to check on a cow.

The afternoon sped by. Luckily, Mrs. Casey had left some cold food for the farmhands' midday meal, but Laura would have to cook dinner herself. After she found some ham out in the smoke house, she made a nice ham bone stew with potatoes and carrots from the cellar. Finishing it off with biscuits should be enough.

Right before dinner, she heard the front door slam.

"Supper will be ready soon. Go get washed up, Pa," she called out. Pa didn't answer.

She turned around and saw Johnny, standing in the kitchen door.

"Well, I ain't your pa," he said grinning. "How are you doing, Laura? I hear you moved out here."

"Just until Mrs. Casey gets better," she answered in a cold voice.

CHAPTER TWENTY-NINE

"Where are the rest of the hands?"

"Oh, they are finishing up. I told them I needed to come in here and get reacquainted with you," he said, inching closer to where she was standing at the stove. "After all, we were nearly sweethearts back at school."

"Johnny, we were not sweethearts and I'm not interested in having a sweetheart out here. I'm just here to help out," she said and turned her back on him.

He walked up to her, standing right behind her. "Well, maybe you came out here 'cause you knew I was here," he whispered in her ear.

Laura turned around and pushed him back.

"Don't get any ideas, Johnny. Get fresh with me and I'll tell my pa and you will be out of a job," she said, eyes blazing.

"Oooh, you've gone and gotten feisty on me!" Johnny said and grabbed her. Laura kneed him and he backed off cursing.

"You'll be a spinster like your old Aunt Beatrice," he spat out. "I was hoping to renew our relationship and save you from all that. But I see you ain't ready yet. You soon will be though. Nights get cold in these parts."

"Good Lord, what is wrong with you? I have no interest in you. I'd rather be a spinster than be with you. Just stay away from me or I swear I will tell Pa." she said. "Now get out of here before I call for him."

"Well, I'll be here when you change your mind," he said, limping out the door.

Dinner was a bit awkward for Laura, but no one seemed to notice. They just talked about the farm and Johnny kept making eyes at her. The other young farm hand looked at him and grinned. She could see Johnny had made up a tall tale about them.

Laura sighed. This was going to be a miserable month, away from Walter, her friends, and sisters. Out here with that creepy Johnny Johnson. But she promised Pa so she would stick with it and not complain. He did so much for all of them. It was the least she could do.

THIRTY

Walter

Walter walked home from work a couple of days later, whistling a tune. Things were going well. He had worked late the past two nights and consequently, received a small raise at the lumber yard. He had a sweetheart—the lovely Laura Watson. Life was good.

As he walked by the general store, he glanced over and saw Addie, waving from the window for him to come into the store. Curious, he walked into the store and took off his hat.

"Hello Miss Addie, is there something I can do for you?" he asked.

"Well, I just wanted to make sure you were all right. I heard about Laura," she said looking sad. "It was quite the shocking news, especially as she seemed to be leading you on."

"What do you mean?" Walter asked.

"Oh, I see no one told you. Well, that's just mean. Anyhow, she moved out to her Pa's farm a few days ago. Her old beau Johnny works out there and I guess she decided to set her cap for him at last. After all, he is a farm hand out there and could take over the farm with her someday. It makes sense. But I know this must be a blow to you." she said, lowering her eyes, trying to look stricken.

Walter could not think of anything to say.

"I'll close up here and we can go get a cup of coffee in the cafe," Addie said. "I'm sure you would like some company right now. I just can't believe she didn't write to you at least."

Addie quickly closed up the store and then took Walter's arm, leading him to the cafe. "Let's just sit in here and have a piece of pie," Addie suggested. "I'll answer any questions you have about Laura and her old beau Johnny."

The two were silent for a while. Finally, Walter asked a question.

"Were they a couple before this?" he asked.

"Oh yes. But Johnny didn't want to get married so Laura decided to make him jealous. I guess it worked. I'm real sorry, Walter." she said, biting her lip.

The two ate their pie in silence. After a while, Addie spoke up.

"I know you must feel bad. I hate to ask, but I wonder if you would do me a favor? It might cheer you up too." Addie said, batting her eyelashes. "My pa wants me to go to the ice cream social at church but I hate to go alone. It's at the Methodist church so none of my friends will go. Would you mind escorting me?"

"I don't know, I guess it would be ok." He looked her in the eyes. "But I'm not ready for a new sweetheart right now. I just want to make that clear."

"Oh, I understand. But I hope you know, not all ladies are as thoughtless as Laura Watson," Addie said. "I certainly would never treat a handsome young man like she treated you."

"I need to go," Walter said, abruptly, standing up. "Thank you Addie."

He walked up to the cashier, paid, and left.

Walter had a miserable week. How could Laura have done this? It didn't seem like her at all. But she was gone, that much was true. He went by her house one day during his lunch break and Mrs. Ware said she had moved out to the farm for a while.

She hadn't left a note or even word for him. What was he supposed to think?

Walter thought about telling Addie he couldn't go to the social. What if Laura changed her mind and came back? He didn't want her to get the impression that he had moved on.

If he didn't hear anything from her by Saturday, he would go to the social with Addie—as a friend.

Saturday came and Walter still hadn't heard anything from Laura. Of course, he didn't have a telephone so she couldn't call him, but she could have written him. He decided to go to the social. Maybe someone there would know what happened.

Walter arrived at the store to escort Addie to the social. When they entered the park, he could see all of Laura's sisters and friends. His heart sank. He thought Addie said they wouldn't be there. He didn't see Laura.

But she has left me without a word, he thought. *I have nothing to feel bad about by escorting Addie.*

Addie hung onto his arm for dear life. She smiled and chatted with him, flirting with all her might. He felt people staring at them, some of them in a mean way. Walking with Addie up to Laura's friend Bessie, he tried to say hello, but she gave him the cold shoulder. Addie steered them away from Laura's friends and after a while, he noticed himself even smiling and laughing with Addie. She was a pretty girl, and made him feel wanted.

When he walked her home, she shivered and asked if he would mind putting his arm around her to warm her up. Even though he felt awkward, he did so. Then Addie snuggled up to him and he began to feel something else. As they reached her door, she clung to him.

"I am having a get together with some friends on Wednesday evening," Addie said, her face close to his. "I wonder if you would come? It's just a casual party. We will meet in our living room upstairs, above the store."

Walter hesitated for just a second. What if Laura changed her mind? He didn't want to lead Addie on. Plus, he didn't want to give up on Laura until he spoke to her.

"Like I said, I'm not ready to court anyone else right now," he said.

"Oh, this wouldn't be like that," Addie said vehemently. "It's just some friends getting together to play games. Please say you'll come!"

Then she moved her lips so close to his that he couldn't help but kiss her. After that kiss he realized that as pretty as she was, he didn't get the same thrill he did when he kissed Laura.

But apparently, Laura was gone.

"Alright. I'll be there," he said, not sure how to get out of it now that he had kissed her.

"Oh, thank you Walter. You won't be sorry," she said, winking at him. "I had a wonderful time tonight. Thank you for being so kind to a lonely girl."

Walter was confused as she didn't seem lonely, but then felt good about helping her. After all, she was the only one to tell him about Laura.

The next day, Susannah called Laura on the telephone out at the farm. When she heard that Laura had left the message with Addie, it all made sense. She decided not to tell Laura about Walter's date with Addie quite yet. She knew Laura couldn't leave and had no way to reach Walter as he had no phone at his aunt's house.

Laura told her about creepy Johnny Johnson and Susannah decided to go find Walter and explain to him what happened.

Unfortunately, every time she had a minute to go see him at the lumber yard he was busy and could not talk. Finally on Wednesday evening she saw him down the street, headed towards the store. Before she could reach him, Addie had grabbed him by the arm and spirited him through the door to her second story home above the mercantile.

Oh dear, Susannah thought. *What do I do now?*

Even though it was not quite closing time, Susannah closed up the store and hurried to Bessie's house. She needed reinforcements.

"What do we do?" she asked Bessie. "Addie is getting her hooks into him. I'm sure she made up some crazy story about why Laura left!"

"Hmmm, isn't tonight the Wednesday monthly game night Addie always has?"

"Yes, but she canceled it. Oh!" Susannah said. "She lured him up there by himself. Her pa is out of town. She'll probably throw herself at him and then he'll have to marry her, as they don't have a chaperone. I doubt he would take advantage of her, but what's to keep her from lying about it?"

"Do you really think she would be that stupid?" Bessie asked. "Why would he marry her if she lied about him?"

"Who knows? But we can't take that chance—we need to get over there right away. Before it's too late!" Susannah cried, wringing her hands.

The two young women walked as quickly as they could and pounded on Addie's door. Soon, Addie opened up the door, looking perturbed.

"What do you want?" she asked in a nasty tone. "I'm busy."

"I'll just bet you are," Bessie said, pushing by Addie. Bessie ran up the stairs and found Walter, alone in the sitting room. Susannah and Addie were hot on her heels.

Walter looked relieved to see Bessie. "Are you here for game night?" he asked.

Both Bessie and Susannah sat down next to Walter who looked at them both, confused. Addie just stood stock still, staring at them.

"I'm not sure what you heard about why Laura isn't in town. Can you tell me?" Susannah asked gently.

All of a sudden, Addie woke up. "Get out of my house!" she screamed. "You aren't welcome here! Walter, don't listen to them. They hate me and don't want me to have you. Everything I told you about Laura was true."

Walter was taken aback. He had never witnessed such a scene before. He looked at Laura's two friends and realized he could find out the truth. The more he thought about it, Addie's story just didn't ring true.

"She moved back to the farm to be with her old beau," he said. "That's what Addie told me. And I never received word from Laura, so I assumed it was true."

Both Bessie and Susannah stared at Addie, openmouthed. This was beyond anything they thought she was capable of.

"First of all, Laura would never break it off with you without talking to you," Susannah said. "She had to leave in a hurry. She told me she left a message with Addie to tell us all that their farm housekeeper was ill and that she needed to go out there to help out. She also said she wrote you a note and left it in Irene's room. Did you get it?"

"No, I didn't," Walter said, staring at Addie. "Why did you tell me that, Addie?"

Addie looked down. "I don't know," she mumbled.

Walter stood up. "I think I need to call Laura. May I use the phone in your store, Addie?"

Addie glared at him. They could tell she wanted to say no. But she couldn't.

"Just make it snappy," Addie answered.

Susannah walked Walter down into the store and Bessie stayed with Addie.

"Addie, why would you do that?" Bessie asked her. "You knew he would find out the truth sooner or later."

"I wanted him! Laura doesn't deserve him. I don't want to marry that dumb Tom Hart. But now I don't have a choice," she whined.

"Why do you have to marry Tom?" Bessie asked, and then it dawned on her. "Addie, you wouldn't have made Walter marry you if you were carrying Tom's child, would you?"

"Well, I would rather be married to Walter than Tom!" Addie said, stomping her foot.

"Does Tom know?" Bessie asked gently. "Come over here and sit down, Addie. Let's figure this out together."

"No, he doesn't. But I guess I'll have to tell him and Daddy too," she said.

The two girls sat together for a while and then Bessie left to go find Tom Hart and send him to Addie.

Walter reached Laura who was horrified by the events but quickly forgave him for escorting Addie. After all, he thought she had thrown him over.

Walter didn't mention that he kissed Addie. He would wait until he saw her in person to confess that.

Walking home that evening, Walter realized something. He loved Laura—he was going to marry her. Nothing was ever going to put that in danger again. He had almost lost the most precious person in his life.

THIRTY-ONE

Laura

As the weeks wore on, Johnny continued to plague Laura. He snuck into the house one afternoon and grabbed her, trying to kiss her. She slapped his face and he retreated, but she knew he'd be back. She finally decided it was time to tell her father. Luckily for Johnny, the next day Mrs. Casey showed up.

"I don't like livin at my sister's. She's so bossy," Mrs. Casey said. "So, you can go on home, Laura. Anyway, I bet ol' Johnny has been botherin' you, yeah? You go on upstairs and pack. I'll find your pa and tell him you need to go."

Laura hugged the sweet old woman and hurried upstairs. She couldn't wait to see Walter.

Before she left, she called and asked Mrs. Ware to ask Irene to look for the note to Walter that had gotten lost. She also asked if Irene could let him know she would be back that evening.

On the way home, Pa told her that he would need to stop at the feed store. He asked if she would pick up some supplies in the general store for the farm kitchen.

"That's fine," Laura said cheerfully. "Then I will get to see Susannah and say hello."

But as she entered the store, she realized that Susannah was not working that day, it was Addie. Mr. Osbourne, her father, was in the store as well.

I'll just have to grit my teeth and act like she doesn't bother me, Laura thought. She was not going to make a scene in front of Addie's father.

As she walked around the store putting items in her basket, Addie approached her.

"Have you heard the news?" Addie simpered. "I'm getting married!"

Laura looked at her in shock.

"You are? When? To whom?"

"Don't worry, it's not Walter," Addie smirked. "Tom Hart and I are getting married next week. It's a very small affair or I would invite you."

Even though the remark about Walter galled her, Laura tried to be gracious.

"That's wonderful. Congratulations, Addie."

"Oh, thank you. I guess I have Walter to thank for this. Tom was absolutely furious about Walter pursuing me and so decided to propose."

Laura could feel her temper starting to rise.

"I believe you tricked Walter into going out with you, Addie. He didn't pursue you," Laura said quietly.

"Well, ok, if that's how you want to see it," Addie replied. "I guess you can have him. He's not that good of a kisser anyway. Not like Tom."

"Excuse me?" Laura said, voice rising.

"Oh, didn't you know? He kissed me after the social last month. Then invited himself over the next week. But by then I had decided on Tom so I had to turn his advances down."

Laura's face burned with fury. "Addie, quit lying. I know he didn't kiss you," she whispered furiously so Mr. Osbourne wouldn't hear her.

"I wouldn't be too sure about that," Addie retorted, and flounced off.

Laura purchased their supplies and got into the wagon as quickly as she could.

"What's a matter Laura?" her Pa asked, seeing her face.

Laura was silent until they were far from the store.

"It's Addie Osbourne," she said furiously. "She is such a—oh, I don't know what!"

"Well, don't let her bother you," Pa said, lowering his voice. "Missy called last night and told me Addie is having to marry Tom Hart real quick. I wouldn't want any of you girls marrying a lazy boy like that. She's gonna have a tough life. And Missy says she'll most likely have a baby pretty soon too."

"Oh," Laura said, realizing that Addie was pregnant. The two were silent for a while.

"Whatever she said, you can be sure it came from jealousy. Try not to react." Pa said.

"But Pa, she said Walter kissed her! I have to know if he did. What if he did? What should I do?"

"Well, if he did it was most likely because that girl manipulated him. Didn't you say she lied to him about you and Johnny? Anyway, that boy Walter is crazy about you. I wouldn't worry too much about it. Even if he did, I'm sure it didn't mean anything," he said firmly.

"I hope you're right," Laura answered.

I wonder if he will tell me? she thought. *If he doesn't, it means I can't trust him. Oh, I hope he does! Unless he didn't do it. But how will I know if he doesn't say anything?*

When they arrived home, Irene followed her up to her bedroom, closed the door, and gave her the note.

"Laura, I'm so sorry this got lost. I know it caused a lot of trouble. Did your friends tell you he went to the social with Addie? Are you through with Walter now?" Irene asked anxiously.

"I'm not sure," Laura answered. "Did you ask him to come over to-night?"

"Yes, he will probably be here right after supper. I'll make sure every-one stays away from the parlor so you can sort this out."

"I hope we can," Laura said. She told Irene what Addie said.

"That Addie!" fumed Irene. "She just wants to make trouble. Did you hear she has to marry that half-wit Tom Hart? I bet she's jealous and wants to ruin things for you."

"Maybe," Laura said. "But if Walter kissed her and doesn't tell me, I don't know what I'll do. I do think I love him, but if he can't be honest with me...."

"But what if he didn't kiss her? Are you going to accuse him of it?"

CHAPTER THIRTY-ONE

Irene worried. "Addie could be lying."

"I don't know!" Laura cried, wringing her hands. "What do I do?"

Irene sat down on the bed next to Laura and put her arm around her. The two sisters were quiet for a while, thinking.

"You will figure it out," Irene said softly. "I know he cares for you, dear sister. But I also know you have to do what you think is best. Let your heart guide you."

Laura sniffed and put her head on Irene's shoulder. They sat there for a while, silently.

Mamie burst in the door, talking a mile-a-minute.

"Hi Laura. I just got home from Doris' house. Did you know Addie is going to get married?" Mamie paused, biting her lip. "Did Irene tell you we saw Walter at the social?"

"Yes, I know all about that," Laura said, getting up to hug Mamie. "Walter is coming over tonight and I hope we can sort it out."

"Now let's get you looking gorgeous so he will be bowled over with your beauty," Irene said. "Why don't you wear your rose-colored dress? You look very desirable in that one!"

"My friend Candance would say you look sultry in that dress," Mamie giggled.

"That's vulgar, Mamie," Irene said.

"Everyone says it!" retorted Mamie.

"But you don't because you have class," Irene answered sharply.

"You're not the boss of me! I swear, ever since you got that boyfriend Carl, you have acted like an old lady," Mamie said.

Laura laughed. "Thank you, for cheering me up, sisters," she said. "I have missed your arguments."

"Happy to help," Mamie said.

"That's what sisters are for," Irene answered.

Irene worked on her hair while Mamie got the wrinkles out of her rose silk dress. They helped her into the dress just in time for dinner. As they walked down the stairs, they heard a knock on the door.

"Oh, no—I can't eat dinner with him until we talk," Laura panicked.

"I'll go see who it is," Irene said. "I can't believe he would get off work this early. Doesn't he usually work until sundown?"

It turned out to be Bessie and Susannah, carrying a big bunch of flowers.

The girls exclaimed over each other and Bessie handed Laura the flowers.

"These are for you from Walter," Bessie said. "He ran into me during his lunch break and asked if I would deliver this bouquet to you this afternoon. It is from his mother's garden."

"Oh—how beautiful. Did he write a card? And how did he know he was going to run into you?" Laura asked.

"He's so romantic," sighed Mamie.

"He was coming to find me at the store," Susannah said. "But Bessie let him know that I didn't work today. It's just as well he didn't go in there and see Addie."

"I'll say," Laura said, frowning.

"He didn't write a card. But he said to tell you welcome home and that he would be here after supper. Now let's go upstairs and catch up," Bessie said.

"You can't—it's time for supper and Mrs. Ware made her special fried chicken for Laura," Irene said. "Of course, she made too much so why don't you stay and eat with us?"

"And I will tell you everything right after dinner," Laura promised.

"Mrs. Ware's fried chicken? Count us in!" Susannah said.

After her friends left, Walter arrived. When Walter walked in the door Laura noticed he seemed nervous. She was nervous too—she had butterflies in her stomach. What if he lied to her or didn't admit it? She would never be able to trust him again. Their romance would be over.

After Joel, Mamie, and Irene said hello to Walter, Irene dragged Mamie upstairs and Joel went into his study and shut the door. Beatrice was at Missy's house for a ladies' supper, so Laura and Walter were alone.

The couple sat in the parlor together on the dark green settee. Laura handed Walter the note and explained how it got lost.

"If only I had gotten this note we could have avoided all of this," he said sadly.

"Avoided all of what?" Laura asked, hesitantly.

Walter sighed and then told her everything about Addie and her scheming—and how he kissed her.

"I'm so sorry, Laura," he said "I was so sad and she was so close to me. I didn't even know it was happening until it was over. But that is no excuse. I will tell you, I felt nothing but regret after I kissed her. It didn't compare to how I feel when I kiss you. I just hope you can forgive me."

Laura stood up, twisting her gloves and pacing. She felt a mixture of both relief that he had been truthful and anger that he had kissed Addie.

"I can't believe you kissed her. Walter, how could you?" she said with a look of hurt on her face.

"I know, I know. I'm such a fool," he said. "I will understand if you want to break it off with me."

"No way will I let Addie come between us. You will just have to find a way to make it up to me," she said fervently.

"Anything—I will do anything! Just name it."

"First of all, come over here and kiss me," she said.

Walter jumped up and walked over to close the parlor door, even though that was not really proper. Laura's eyes grew wide. He then took Laura in his arms and kissed her with more passion than he ever had before.

He took her by the hand and led her to the settee. He pulled her onto his lap and they continued to lose themselves in each other's arms, kissing and caressing each other. As they became more and more heated, they both began losing all sense of where they were.

Finally, there was a noise outside the room and they sprang apart, jumping up. They looked at each other, breathing hard, and then laughed.

"Wait! I forgot I was mad at you. How do I know you will never do this again?" Laura said sternly.

"Oh, Laura," Walter said looking into her eyes. "Like I said, I regretted that kiss every moment since then. I will never hurt you like that again; I promise. I'm so very sorry."

"Well, I guess I forgive you," Laura said. "But only if you kiss me like that more often."

"That's a promise," Walter whispered. "But I must go before someone comes in here. What would your father say?"

Walter then took her hands and looked at her tenderly.

"Laura, thank you for forgiving me. I love you," he said earnestly.

"Oh, Walter, I love you too," she said, eyes shining.

Walter kissed her once more. "I will see you tomorrow. I don't think I can stay away. And one day, we will marry. I promise you."

"Oh yes," she whispered. "It's all I dream of."

As Walter left the room, Laura sank back into the settee, filled with wonder. He said he loved her! And oh my, how she loved him.

She knew now what she wanted for the rest of her life. It was Walter. The best part was that he wanted her too.

THIRTY-TWO

Beatrice

Beatrice was thirty and officially a spinster. She continued to live at Joel's house and help with the girls, who needed a mother more than ever. Both Laura and Irene had beaus, and needed someone to keep an eye on them. Mamie's girlfriends did nothing but giggle over boys, so Beatrice wanted to keep a sharp eye on Mamie too. She was busy.

In truth, that was just an excuse. Beatrice had never really found a man that interested her. She preferred the company of women, so she belonged to the Young Ladies Auxiliary at church. They mostly just met and gossiped, but sometimes helped with projects in town, especially with the school. That helped to keep her busy as well. But she was lonely. She started to wonder if she would ever find love.

One spring day in 1911, Beatrice went into the new milliner's shop, Miss Millicent's Fashions, ostensibly to look for a new hat. She had heard that the woman who owned the shop was very fashionable and came from New York City. She was dying to meet someone who had lived in New York.

I bet she is very sophisticated, she thought. *But why on earth would she ever want to move to this little town?*

Beatrice entered the shop and saw that the owner—she assumed her name was Millicent—was busy with Addie Hart, who was visibly pregnant. Addie was telling the shopkeeper why she did not like the hat in the shop window. As the two women chatted, Beatrice looked around the shop.

The shop had tasteful white flocked wallpaper and several small dressing tables against the walls, each with a large gold-framed looking glass. The white painted tables had gold silk skirts. The stools in front of each table were upholstered with a chic blue, white, and gold-colored fabric. There was a lovely oriental rug on the floor.

One large table had many rolls of ribbons displayed—Beatrice had never seen such a variety of colorful ribbons, some with stripes, with flowers, and vibrant jacquard and geometric designs. There were grosgrain ribbons in a multitude of bright hues, shiny silk ribbons in jewel tones, delicate lace ribbons of all shades and colors.

Of course, there were hats everywhere. Hats on stands, on the walls, on tables. Hats with feathers, with large flowers, hats with plain ribbons and with fancy bows. Beatrice removed her gloves to touch the ostrich feathers on a huge straw hat. She had never seen such beautiful hats before—at least not in Tethertown. It was an elegant and feminine shop.

"Those feathers are so ostentatious!" Addie declared. "Why, no one would be caught dead wearing that hat in this town. I think you should change it."

Beatrice saw a look of doubt cross Millicent's face. Without even thinking, she jumped in.

"Oh my, I was just hoping to try that hat on!" she said. "Please don't change it."

"I will be happy to let you try it on," Millicent said, smiling at Beatrice. "After all, it is the latest fashion from Paris. If you will please just take a seat, I will help you once I am finished with this young lady."

Addie sniffed and started barking out orders for the hat she wanted Millicent to create for her. Beatrice noticed how patient Millicent was with Addie. She also noticed how beautiful and elegant Millicent was.

I wonder if she's married? Beatrice thought.

After about twenty minutes, Addie finished ordering the hat and left. Beatrice smiled at Millicent.

"Young Addie can be quite a challenging girl to deal with. Luckily, she's one of a kind in this town."

"Oh, I don't mind," the shopkeeper said politely. "I worked in a shop in New York and had many spirited young ladies to deal with. It is part of the job. Now, shall I fetch the hat in the front window?"

"Oh yes, I would love to have a beautiful hat to wear. All of my hats are a bit conservative. But of course, we have never had such a fashionable place to shop in our little town before this. Your shop is beautiful, as are your hats," Beatrice said.

"Thank you. I'm sure you must be wondering why I would move here to open a shop all the way from New York," Millicent said as she got the hat out of the window.

"Well, yes. I did wonder why you would choose such a small town for your shop. I don't know how many women in this little town have much fashion sense—apart from Addie, of course. I just assumed your husband wanted to move here?"

"No, I'm not married. It's a long story. Perhaps I will tell you someday." She placed the hat on Beatrice's head. "Now, what do you think of this creation? I think it suits you well."

Beatrice was shocked by how smart she looked in the beautiful hat.

"Ooooh, I love it," she said, turning from side to side. "But I imagine it's pretty dear. I have a limited budget."

"I'll tell you what," Millicent said. "Take me to lunch wearing this hat and I will give you a twenty percent discount. It will be like free advertising for me."

"Why, I would love to," Beatrice said, beaming.

Millicent put a sign in the window, locked the door and the two ladies had a nice lunch at the cafe. Several women stopped to admire Beatrice's new hat during their meal. Millicent offered to set up special appointments for each of them to try and find their own style.

"You are a pretty shrewd businesswoman," Beatrice remarked as they left the cafe. "Now those ladies will spread the word about having their own personal milliner in town. That was brilliant."

"Well, that was a nice bonus to the meal. But really, I just wanted to make a friend. Would your husband or beau mind if you spent time with a single lady sometimes?" Millicent asked shyly.

"Considering I have neither, no problem," Beatrice answered.

"I would love to cook you a nice dinner but alas, I am staying at the boarding house. I was hoping to find a nice little room to rent with a kitchen, but haven't found one in my price range."

"Instead, you can come over to my house and eat dinner with me," Beatrice suggested. "We can eat a late dinner and shoo all my nieces and brother-in-law away. I'll ask our housekeeper, Mrs. Ware, to make her special chicken. What do you think?"

"It sounds like fun, but don't shoo your family away. I would love to get to know them. It would be such a treat eating dinner with them all. It's been pretty lonely at the boarding house."

"OK, if you say so," Beatrice said doubtfully. "It can get pretty lively at our table at times. The girls like to bicker. I'll try and make sure they behave, but no guarantees."

"Don't do that on my account! I miss my big family. I have two sisters and two brothers myself. We had a few disagreements at the supper table over the years."

Lying in bed that night, Beatrice kept thinking about Millicent. Something about her was so sweet and kind. And she was so beautiful. Beatrice got a funny feeling when she thought about Millicent's trim little figure.

It's almost as if I was attracted to her, she thought.

She remembered feeling that way about a classmate named Minnie when she was sixteen. Beatrice had a beau at the time, but she had actually felt more comfortable with Minnie than she did with him. She and Minnie even kissed on a dare at a sleepover one night. Minnie laughed and pushed her away, but Beatrice had felt something different—a strong attraction. She wanted to kiss her again.

As she turned over in bed, she recalled that over the years she would feel attracted to other women, but just wrote it off as loneliness. She just could not seem to find a man she liked. But now she was starting to wonder. Was she more attracted to women than men?

Oh my, maybe I do feel something for Millicent, she realized. It was strange. Did other women feel this way? If so, no one had ever said anything.

As Beatrice thought more about Millicent, she started to squirm. Soon she was pleasuring herself, just thinking about how Millicent had brushed up against her when they said goodbye at the hat shop. When she finished, she knew she would have to go see her the next day. She would not be able to stay away.

As the weeks went on, Beatrice found a reason to stop in and say hello to Millicent almost every day. Many days they would eat lunch together, although with more and more business, sometimes Millicent wasn't able even to eat lunch.

"You need an assistant. What if I helped out every day for just a few hours?" Beatrice suggested. "Then you could go get lunch, have time to order supplies, put new hats together, and do whatever you don't have time for now. You wouldn't have to pay me. I would just do it for fun."

"Oh, would you?" Millicent asked, looking relieved. "I thought about asking you but did not want to presume that you might want to work in a shop. I would be so grateful, and will pay you the same I was making in New York City."

"No, don't use up all your profits on me. You'll never be able to rent a house if you don't save your money. I'll find out how much Mr. Osborne pays Laura's friend Susannah in the general store, and perhaps you can match that. That would be more in keeping with Tethertown. We don't live in a big city, after all."

"I would be so grateful," Millicent said again. "When can you start?"

"How about today, after a celebratory lunch? But I do have one more request for you," Beatrice said. "Will you tell me why you left New York?"

"After work, let's go for a walk in the park and I will tell you the story," Millicent said.

The two ladies dashed out for a quick lunch. Millicent spent the rest of the afternoon showing Beatrice how to ring up sales and how to do some of the basic tasks. Near closing time, two ladies came in from the town of St. Joseph.

"We heard about your shop with the latest fashions from New York and Paris," one of them told Millicent. "We don't have any fashionable Milliners in St. Jo."

The ladies bought two hats each. As they left, Millicent thanked them and asked them to send their friends.

"Oh, we will," they assured her.

After they were gone, Millicent locked the door. The ladies hugged each other in celebration.

"What an amazing day!" Millicent declared. "My new best friend comes to work with me, and my new clientele will spread the word of my shop. I'm on my way!"

Millicent hugged Beatrice again, but this time it felt different. They both hesitated, looking at each other, and then Millicent took Beatrice by the hand and led her to the back room. She cupped Beatrice's face in her hands and kissed her slowly.

Beatrice felt something she never felt before—true desire. As she kissed Millicent back, she realized she wanted more. She wanted to feel Millicent's creamy skin, her breasts. She wanted to drown in her body. She wanted Millicent to touch her, all over.

Millicent slowly undressed Beatrice and then herself while Beatrice watched in awe. On the shabby old chaise lounge, Beatrice finally learned what real love was—what it felt like.

It was ecstasy.

Millicent brought her to climax, then showed her how she wanted Beatrice to pleasure her. Beatrice was in heaven. Never could she have imagined feeling like this. She could not get enough of kissing Millicent's breasts, her navel and oh, tasting her "Venus' cradle" as Millicent called it.

When the two lovers came up for air, they realized it was dark outside.

"Will your family be missing you?" Millicent asked, as they got dressed.

"I don't know, nor do I care. I just want to stay here and be with you. Oh, Millicent, I never knew it could be like this." Beatrice said, eyes filling. "I'm so happy, but so scared. Is something wrong with me—with us?"

Millicent sat down and gently took Beatrice by the hand. "Some women are like this. I don't know if we are wrong, but this is what I am. I didn't choose this, it is just how I feel. In some places, we could be arrested if we were caught. So we have to be careful if we want to do this again."

"Oh, yes, I do want to do this again! I didn't even know this was possible—to be with another woman, I mean." Beatrice stammered. "Sometimes I had feelings for other girls, but it was confusing. I knew I was supposed to have those feelings for men, but I never did."

"We can talk about it tomorrow. It's getting late. I think we should go home and rest. Will you come to work tomorrow?"

"Yes, I will."

"Then tomorrow night after work we will talk, and I will tell you all about how I ended up in Tethertown," Millicent promised.

"Will we be able to be with each other again?" Beatrice asked.

"Only if you want to. But again, we need to be discreet. I can't stress that enough," Millicent said firmly. "Now go home!" And she shoved her gently out the door.

As she walked home, Beatrice was full of wonder. *I think I am in love. I am so happy*, she thought.

As she got close to home, she stopped.

How will I ever keep this a secret—especially from my family? she thought. *They'll see it all over my face. I must calm down.*

She sat on a nearby bench and took a few deep breaths. She thought about what Millicent said about being discreet.

She remembered how folks talked about Ray Smart and his friend George Smyth who lived together in a small house out of town. Some people said they were a couple, which was confusing as they were both men. But she saw how folks judged them for it. When she asked Joel about it one day, he said it was a shame that folks were so small minded. He said they were not even welcome at church, which he thought was wrong. He never really explained why people judged them so harshly.

Maybe she was like them, only liking women. She shuddered to think what people would say if they found out. Yes, they would need to be discreet.

After a few minutes, she went inside the house. The girls were already upstairs, Joel was in the parlor. Beatrice apologized to Joel for missing dinner, told him quickly about her new job, and then went into the kitchen to grab some food. Mrs. Ware was already in bed, so Beatrice took her food upstairs to eat in her room.

She worried she would not be able to sleep, but as soon as she finished eating, she fell dead asleep.

The next day was a busy one. They had so many clients that they didn't even have time to talk. Beatrice had to run out to get them lunch and bring it back to the shop.

When she was at the cafe waiting for the food, she saw Susannah and inquired about how much she made at the general store.

"I only get twelve cents per hour," she grumbled. "I think he would have to pay a man more than that, which is probably why he hired me. Why?"

"I am going to work at the new milliner shop in town," Beatrice answered. "I need something to do and I really like the owner, Millicent Cavanaugh."

Beatrice blushed when she realized what she'd said. But seeing Susannah's reaction, she relaxed. *No one would ever guess what we had been doing*, she thought.

Beatrice could hardly wait until the shop closed. The minute Millicent locked the door, the ladies hurried into the back room for more passionate lovemaking. After their steamy encounter, Millicent suggested they go to dinner at the Cafe.

"After all, we have so much to celebrate!" she said, winking at Beatrice.

Walking in the park after dinner, Millicent explained what had happened to make her move from New York.

"I had become engaged to Marvin, a man my mother had picked out for me. But in the meantime, I started having romantic liaisons with one of the girls in my employer's milliner shop. One day, our boss caught us kissing in the backroom. She fired me immediately," she said sadly.

"Soon after, my grandfather died. He left me some money and the deed to this building. So I wrote to his lawyer, who hired a man to fix up the shop. I broke up with Marvin and then moved here. I used most of my money from Grandpa for train fare, furniture, decorating the shop and for millinery supplies. That is why I can't rent a house yet."

"Who was your grandfather, and why did he leave it to you? Shouldn't he have given it to his own son or daughter?"

"I was always his favorite grandchild because I paid attention to him, wrote to him, and even visited him here once. I knew all about Tethertown before I moved here. I always loved it here," she sighed. "His name was P.C. Warren."

"I knew him. He was such a nice man. He was a widower, right? Lived on Front Street?"

"Yes. The proceeds from his house went to his daughter, my mother. She always hated Tethertown, so she never would have moved here. I wish I could have bought it from her, or at least rented it. But she was so mad about my getting fired, breaking off my engagement, and moving here that she refused to help me."

"Did she know why you were fired?"

"I told her that they didn't need me anymore, that business was bad. But she knew that wasn't true. I imagine she suspected the truth about me a long time ago, which was why she insisted I become engaged to that dolt Marvin."

"Thanks for telling me," Beatrice answered.

"I will need to find a house to rent pretty soon," Millicent said. "I hate the boarding house, and I don't think we should use our place of business for our 'meetings' anyway. That just doesn't feel right."

"Hmm. Well, I have quite a lot of money that was left to me when my mother died," Beatrice said thoughtfully. "Joel has been after me to invest it into real estate. What if I bought or built a house and you rented it from me?"

"No, no, that wouldn't do," Millicent said. "I can't rent from you if you are my employee, not to mention my lover! No, no. I will find a place at some point."

"I can ask Joel to help you find a place," Beatrice offered. "He is so glad I found a new friend."

"Oh, is he?" Millicent asked in a wry tone. "I don't know how happy he'd be if he knew what kind of friend I was."

"I think he would understand," Beatrice said slowly. "You know he has been having an affair with my Aunt Missy since soon after my sister died. They never married, but are still engaged, as far as I know."

"Really? Those two seem so circumspect," Millicent said. "Perhaps I can come to dinner next week, and I can ask him for help."

"Great idea!"

. . .

With his many connections in town, Joel was able to find a small one-bedroom house close by for Millicent to rent. Over the next few months, Beatrice spent more and more time after work at Millicent's house.

Their passion for each other grew. On slow days, they had a hard time keeping their hands off of each other in the back room. Some nights they hurried to close up, then walked separately to Millicent's place, where they spent hours exploring and pleasuring each other. Other nights, Beatrice would go home for dinner, and then sneak out later for a tryst with Millicent. She was always careful to walk there alone, usually under cover of darkness.

One night after a steamy encounter at Millicent's place, Joel asked to speak to her. Heart racing, she came into Joel's study and sat down.

Is he going to ask me about Millicent? she wondered nervously.

After she sat down in a leather chair in the well-appointed study, she looked down at her hands. Joel cleared his throat and she looked up at him. He was smiling at her, and she felt her fears melt away.

"I am so happy you are enjoying your work at the millinery. It occurred to me the other day that perhaps you might think about building a house," he said. "It would be a great investment, a place for you to rent out or to live in someday."

He paused. "We love having you here, of course, but I wonder if you would prefer having your own home at some point. What do you think?"

"Won't it be a scandal, a single woman living alone?"

"I take it you don't ever intend to marry?" he asked, eyeing her curiously.

"No, I don't think so." she answered quickly.

"Well, I wouldn't worry what everyone thinks," he said. "It's none of their business. You deserve to have your own place—if you want it."

I should have known he would support me no matter what, she thought.

"Thanks so much, Joel," she said. "I think it would be nice to build a place to live in someday. But I want to stay here until Mamie turns eighteen, at least. She still needs me."

Joel abruptly changed the subject. "I like Millicent. And I'm glad you have someone you care about."

Beatrice searched his face to see if he understood.

He smiled at her. "It is kind of like Missy and me, right? And it's nobody's business. The important thing is your happiness. That's all that matters to your family," he said gently.

Beatrice looked worried. "Does Missy know?"

"Yes. She is also glad you found Millicent. You lost your mother, your home, your sister, and have worked so hard for all of us. You deserve whatever happiness comes your way."

"I do love her, you know. It must seem strange to you that I could love a woman. But I do. And she loves me too, I think."

"Well, I can understand your love for a woman. I loved Belle so much, and love Missy too. Love is good, no matter who it is for."

"I love you, Joel. You have been such a good brother. I am so lucky," she said, smiling at him.

"I love you too, dear sister. And remember to bring Millicent here any time, no forewarning necessary. We will treat her like family."

"You already do. Thank you for being so understanding," she said with tears in her eyes, and kissed his weathered cheek.

"Just as you have always been understanding with me. Now I must go—I am late for my date with Missy. Good night!" And Joel hurried out the front door.

THIRTY-THREE

Laura

Before Laura knew it, it was 1912. Of course, being in love with Walter made each day exciting. He was now twenty-two, and talking about setting up a home for them someday.

Although not officially engaged, Laura felt sure it was only a matter of time until he proposed. Of course, he needed to get a promotion at the lumber yard first. His current salary would not support a family. They would have to be patient.

Laura was not a very patient person. She complained to her sisters, her friends, and even her father about the fact that it would probably be a very long time until Walter got paid enough to support a wife and family. They had been "stepping out" for two years now. She was tired of waiting.

In the meantime, her sister Irene became engaged to her beau Carl Reade. She had pined for Willy for so long, but finally realized that he did not feel the same way. Once she met Carl, she realized that what she felt for Willy was just a school girl crush.

When Willy turned twenty-one, he moved to Montana, to the town where he was born. Carl quickly became the man she wanted to marry. Now, most likely, Irene would marry before Laura.

"At this rate, Mamie will beat me to the altar," Laura groused to her Aunt Beatrice.

Mamie also had a serious beau, even though she was barely sixteen. His name was Jim Baker and he was a young up-and-coming banker in town. They would not have to wait until he had more money to marry. But Pa wouldn't hear of an engagement to Jim Baker until she was seventeen.

"Now Laura, you know this is not a race," her Aunt Beatrice chided. "Walter is a fine man, worth waiting for. He will figure it out. You don't want to marry and be dirt poor, like that silly Addie Hart."

"That's true," Laura agreed. "I never could figure out why she went out with that dumb Tom Hart in the first place."

"Well, Addie had a reputation." Beatrice said. "Beggars can't be choosers. She also had a baby pretty soon after the wedding. You must not make the same mistake Addie made, Laura. Wait for your wedding night."

"But sometimes I think I shall burst if we can't be together soon! I love him so much."

"You sound just like your ma did when your father was courting her. I remember it well. You know, my pa was against her marrying your dad for so long because your dad was poor. But things worked out for them, and things will work out for Walter and you too, you'll see," Beatrice said.

"Didn't you ever want to marry?" Laura asked.

"No, I never met a man I could love enough," Beatrice sighed. "But I'm happy with my life—you girls, your Pa, my job, and my dear friend Millicent. And now I'm thinking of building a house that I can move into once you girls are all out of the house. My life is just like I want it."

"Well, mine isn't," Laura complained. "I wish there was a better solution for us instead of waiting for Walter to get a big enough raise for us to marry."

That night at dinner, Joel came in late. He walked into the dining room in a huff and apologized for his tardiness.

"I had to change a tire on the way home so I'll need to wash up."

After a few minutes Joel sat down at the table and began to eat. He was very quiet, a sure sign that something went wrong.

"What is bothering you, Joel?" Beatrice asked. "You are awfully quiet."

"My foreman Mr. Johnson quit," he complained. "Says he's done with farm work and wants to take his son Johnny and move out west to California. To do what, he doesn't know. He's a fool. But now I'm in a pickle. I don't know anyone available to do the job, which means I need to move out to the farm starting tomorrow."

"Oh no, Pa!" cried the girls in a chorus.

Thank goodness Johnny is leaving, thought Laura.

"Dear me," said Beatrice. "Well, let's put our heads together after dinner and see if we can come up with a better solution."

After the girls went upstairs, Beatrice knocked on his study door.

He called her in and she sat down.

"I have an idea that could kill two birds with one stone," she said.

Joel perked up. "I'd love to hear it."

"Why not hire Walter as a hand, train him, and then let him take over when he's ready? He worked with his father's cattle in Kentucky. Laura and he are waiting to marry until he has enough money for a home. They could live in the farmhouse once you promote him to foreman. What do you think?"

"Well, it's an idea," Joel said thoughtfully. "But what happens if he is not suited for the job? I hate to get their hopes up."

"Take him on a trial basis. Give him six months and see where he is. Would you know by then if he could do the job?" she asked.

"Perhaps," he said. "Let me talk to Walter and see what he thinks. Don't say anything to Laura yet. He may not want to move so far out of town from Laura and his mother, anyway."

"All right," she said. "When will you talk to him?"

"I'll go speak to him before I leave tomorrow. I'll let him tell Laura if he's willing."

"Sounds like a plan," Beatrice said smiling. "I hope it works out."

Walter

Early the next morning, Joel found Walter walking to work. He explained his proposal for the farm.

Walter was beyond thrilled. "When can I start?" he asked.

"As soon as possible," Joel answered. "You understand you are on a trial basis for the foreman job? It will take at least six months to a year before you are ready, if the job even suits you. In the meantime, you will need to live in the bunkhouse with Hap and George. We are down a farmhand as Johnny left, so I'll be out there as foreman for a while. You will have Sundays off unless there is an emergency. You won't be able to come into town and see Laura and your mother but once a week."

"I have a feeling Laura will want to move out to the farm, then. What did she say?" Walter asked.

"I have not told her. That's up to you."

But what about George or Hap? Don't they want to be foreman?" I would hate to step on their toes," Walter said.

"Hap isn't ready for that and George plans on moving to California himself someday. Anyhow, I'd rather the farm was run by a family member, which I assume you will be before too long, am I right?" Joel looked at Walter with a piercing gaze. He still remembered Laura's tears when she heard about Addie.

"Yes, sir. I wondered if I could ask for Laura's hand. We won't marry until I'm established at the farm as a foreman. But I would like to propose."

Joel paused for a moment, thinking.

"You have my blessing," Joel finally answered.

"Thank you, sir. I won't let you down."

"Just see that you don't let my daughter down," Joel said.

"Oh no sir, I won't. I love her and will take care of her," Walter said earnestly.

"All right then. Well, I need to get going. Please just ride out when you are ready. I realize you will need to talk to your boss at the lumber yard and let Laura and your mother know."

The day was a whirlwind for Walter. His boss was disappointed to lose him, but understood, gave him his pay, and wished him well.

Next, he went to Laura's house to tell her. She was thrilled.

"Oh, Walter! This is everything I hoped for," she cried out in joy.

"I must prove myself so your Pa will make me foreman," he said. "I'll be very busy so I will only be able to come in town to see you once a week.'

"Oh no you won't see me only once a week. I am moving out to the farm. I'm sure the new housekeeper would like the help and I don't want to be away from you," she said throwing her arms around him.

Walter promised to be back Sunday to help her move her things out to her new home. He had a plan to propose to her at the farm on Sunday, but first he would need to get a ring.

With that in mind, he kissed her goodbye and went to the general store to talk to Susannah about the best way to go about procuring a ring that he could afford. She suggested that Joel should order one from the jeweler in St Joseph. She promised to go look at them for him that very afternoon, then write and let him know what they had in his price range.

"I know the owner well so I'll see if he will let me bring some rings here for you to choose from," she promised. "What stone do you think you want in the ring?"

"I don't know. I will have to see what they cost. I have my wages and a small inheritance from my father, so I know I can't spend more than $30.00. I appreciate your help with this," Walter said.

All he had left to do was to go home, tell his mother, pack up his few belongings, and ride out to the farm.

His mother was happy for him, especially with the thought of him back on a farm.

"Work hard, my son, just like your father taught you," she said as he was leaving. Then she kissed his cheek.

Finally, he rode up to the farm. It was a beautiful, well-maintained place and he felt a thrill when he realized it would be his home. Glancing around, he saw quite a few head of cattle, a milk cow, chickens, and horses.

The main house took his breath away. It was a beautiful white clapboard house with a wrap-around porch. He couldn't even imagine living in such a grand place.

Walter made his way to the bunkhouse, which was clean and comfortable. He met the farmhands and jumped into the work right away.

The week flew by. Walter enjoyed working with Joel, Hap, and George. He worked as hard as he could and loved every second.

This is what I was meant to do, he realized. He was a farmer, just like his father before him.

He received a letter from Susannah on Friday suggesting two rings in his price range. She had written detailed descriptions and drawn pictures of them. She had brought them both to the general store. He could pay her, and she would return the other ring and money to the jeweler.

Walter chose the ruby ring. The other ring had a large, single pearl. He thought Laura would prefer the small but bright red ruby. It seemed more romantic to him. After all, red was the color of love.

On Sunday morning, he rode into town with Joel as they were moving Laura out to the farm. Laura would bring all or most of her clothes, books, and mementoes—like the only photograph she had of her mother. All of that would not fit in the buggy, so they brought the wagon.

After Walter met Susannah at the store and purchased the ring, he could hardly contain himself. He couldn't wait to see the look on Laura's face when she saw the ring. He knew she would love it. His plan had been to ask Laura to marry him once they got to the farm. Now he wondered if she would rather be in town for that so she could show the ring off to her sisters and friends who were coming over for a farewell supper at noon. Perhaps he would ask her to go for a walk in the park after they packed up the wagon and he would propose to her there. Plus, he didn't think he could wait much longer. He longed to kiss her and make her his.

As they walked home together after church, he realized he could not wait. When they came close to the park, he asked Laura if she would come and sit in the gazebo with him for a minute. The park was deserted as most folks were still in church.

In the gazebo, he knelt down and asked if she would marry him.

"Yes, I will," Laura said, with tears in her eyes. When he gave her the ring, she gasped.

"It's perfect—so beautiful!" she exclaimed, as he slipped it on her finger. "Where did you get it?"

Walter told her the story of how Susannah helped him purchase the ring.

"What a good friend she is," Laura said, smiling.

"I thought we could marry next summer. I need to get my feet under me at the farm and see if I can handle the foreman's job. I think I can, but I have a lot to learn," Walter said.

"I know you can!" Laura looked up at him. "Oh Walter, I am so happy, and can't wait to be married to you."

Walter looked around. Seeing no one, he kissed her passionately.

"It will be hard to wait, " he whispered. "But I have to be settled first."

"Of course," she said.

They kissed again, then walked to the house to share their news with everyone.

THIRTY-FIVE

Laura

Later that afternoon when they arrived at the farm, Laura bustled inside to put away her things and to make a small dinner for them. When she saw the kitchen, her heart sank. Mrs. Casey had finally decided to move to her sister's house for good, and the new housekeeper and cook, Mrs. Olson, had not been doing a good job keeping things clean. It was Sunday, so she would not be back until tomorrow. Laura would have to talk to her.

After Laura put her things away, she cleaned the kitchen and started making a chicken pie with biscuits on top. Before she knew it, she had four hungry men at her table, and then it was time to clean up.

Walter stayed behind to help her. The couple worked side-by-side and were done in no time.

"I best go to the bunkhouse," Walter said after the kitchen was clean. "Tomorrow is an early day. But first I need to do something."

"What's that?" Laura asked.

"Just this," he said, and kissed her passionately. "Goodnight, sweet Laura," he whispered. "I love you!" And off he went.

. . .

Life on the farm was hard. Laura had forgotten how many chores there were. She took over care of the chickens, gathering eggs, milking their cow, and keeping the house clean. She asked Mrs. Olson to cook and to do all the kitchen work—keep it clean—and do the laundry, along with

Laura's help. Mrs. Olson did not live far away, so she went home after she cooked dinner every night. Laura and Walter cleaned up. It was their time to be alone together.

Walter seemed to be doing well. He certainly loved the work and the farm. Pa didn't say how he thought Walter was faring, and Laura did not want to ask. But it seemed that all was well.

Some weeks Irene, and Mamie came out to the farm to stay for a few days. It was like old times. Even though her mother had been gone for so long, Laura still missed her, especially when they were all together. She had only a few memories of her, but those were precious to her. She wished so much she could talk to her.

Soon Laura would have to move back into town for a few weeks to help Irene get ready for her wedding to Carl. Irene's wedding was to be a lavish affair with four bridesmaids, groomsmen, and a big reception at the Grange. Irene had gone to St. Joseph to purchase a beautiful lace wedding dress with a train and long veil. The latest fashion in weddings was to have a lunchtime wedding, with cake and punch at the reception. But Irene decided to serve little sandwiches as well, which would have to be made the morning before the wedding.

Carl also wanted a wedding dinner for both families, which would take place at his parents' home. There was a lot to do. Mrs. Olson agreed to help Mrs. Ware and Carl's mother with all the food.

"We are not having a big wedding like this!" Laura said to Walter during their dinnertime cleanup after her sisters had left the farm. "This is so expensive, and too much work."

"I agree," Walter said. "I think Carl's position in town is why they are putting on such a big wedding. He's hoping it gets in the St. Joseph paper as well, which could drum up more business for him."

"I just want to be married to you," Laura said. "When do you think Pa will let you know? It's been four months."

"We have to get through the haying season and the cattle auction. He needs to see if I can handle all of that. If I do all right, then I think I will get the job," Walter answered.

The next two months went by slowly for Laura. Irene's wedding went off without a hitch. Mamie turned seventeen and became engaged to Jim Baker. Walter did well with the haying, and the auction was coming up soon.

The night before the auction, Pa asked to speak to Laura and Walter after dinner.

"You have done a wonderful job on the farm, Walter," Joel started. "I have every confidence the auction will go well. I think it is time for you to take on the position of foreman."

"Thank you, sir," Walter said.

"Oh, Pa! Thank you!" Laura cried and went over to kiss him.

"I am going to move out of the big bedroom and I think you should move in there, Laura. I'll go into one of the smaller rooms. It makes sense, because I plan to move back to town anyway. I know that the farm will be in good hands," he said with a smile, and left the room.

Walter came and knelt down in front of her. "Shall we get married tomorrow?" he asked.

"I think we may have to wait until I can get myself ready," Laura said. "I want to wear my mother's dress, and I will have to alter it. I'd like to get married in the church, just with our families and a couple of friends. Would that be all right with you? Could we have our wedding in two weeks?"

"Yes, my dear. But no longer! I cannot wait to really hold you in my arms in our wedding bed," he whispered in her hair, holding her close.

A week before the wedding, Laura realized she was nervous about the wedding night.

She finally went to her Aunt Beatrice for advice.

"I don't know what to do," she said. "I am so afraid of disappointing him."

"Don't worry, you and Walter will figure it out. And you can't disappoint him. He loves you and you love him. Everything will be fine," Beatrice assured her. "Do you know what happens?"

"Well, I have seen animals on the farm . . ."

"It's not quite the same. But as I said, you will figure it out. And I hear it is wonderful—the very best part of marriage. Anyway, that is what I overheard my mother telling your mother before her wedding, many years ago," Beatrice said.

Two weeks later, with only close friends and family in attendance, Laura was married in her mother's wedding dress on a beautiful July morning. They had a small lunch with family and friends at Joel's home in Tethertown, then rode back to the farm to start their life together.

Walter did the chores when they arrived home. He had Mrs. Olson serve dinner to the farmhands in the bunkhouse and Laura cooked them a simple meal so they could be alone.

After dinner, they sat on the front porch, chatting about the wedding and their plans for their future.

"I'd like to get a gas-powered truck someday," Walter said. "It would make our farm more efficient, and we could grow more hay."

"Ummm, yes," Laura answered. She tried to concentrate on what he was saying, but she was starting to get anxious.

Finally, Walter looked at her and realized that she was worried. "Let's go upstairs, shall we?" he smiled.

"It's not quite sunset yet," Laura said.

"That's all right. Come, take my hand. It's time, my darling."

Upstairs, Walter asked if he could help her to undress. Laura nervously agreed.

Laura looked into his eyes and realized that this was Walter—the man she had loved and longed to be with for so long. Her nervousness went away.

Walter began by kissing her passionately. His mouth moved down to her shoulders, where he began to unbutton her dress. He helped her to take off the dress, then began kissing the tops of her breasts. He undid the laces of her corset, pulled it off and began cupping and then sucking on her nipples. Laura groaned and he bent down to slowly remove her stockings and gently pull off her pantaloons. He quickly removed his shirt and pants and led her to the bed. They laid down facing each other, Walter began to caress her body gently. She lost herself in the feeling of his touch and the sensation of his mouth, kissing her all over.

Laura rolled on top of him, kissing him passionately. Soon they were both panting, wanting more. Walter rolled her over and moved his mouth down her belly while using his hands to move her legs apart. As he caressed her, she began to moan softly. He placed his finger inside her, and she opened her eyes in surprise.

"Does that feel good?" he whispered.

"Oh, yes," she whispered back.

Laura groaned and asked what Walter wanted her to do.

"Open your legs and relax," he said softly. "This may hurt a bit and it will bleed some, so I've been told. I guess only the first time is like that, though."

After he slowly moved into her, Laura, who was slick and felt ready, put her hands on his buttocks and pushed him deeper inside her. It hurt a bit but then, it felt delicious. Soon Walter climaxed and then rolled off of her and took her in his arms.

"Are you feeling alright?" he asked.

"It hurts a bit," she admitted. "But I liked it."

"I hope so," Walter said. "I have been told that it won't hurt as much the next time, and then we will get to the place where it only feels good. Now, let me see if I can bring you to a climax."

"No, I think we should just sleep now. I am a bit tender down there," she said.

"We'll wait until you feel better before we go again," he promised. "I want you to enjoy our love making too, not just get through it."

"Oh Walter, did you think that was what I was doing? That could not be further from the truth. It did hurt but that's just because it was the first time. I still loved being with you like that," she said earnestly.

The next morning, Laura woke up before dawn and snuggled next to her new husband. She wanted to see if they could make love again. She began caressing his chest and he opened his eyes and groaned. This time was quicker and more intense. It still hurt a bit, but not too badly.

Afterwards, smiling at his beautiful bride, Walter said quietly, "I need to go do some farm chores." He kissed her gently. "Now, go back to sleep, my bride. Mrs. Olson has strict instructions to treat you like a guest this week. Just come downstairs when you are hungry."

Laura lay in bed, stretched, and then fell back to sleep, still glowing from their lovemaking.

. . .

Their first year of marriage was a busy but joyous one. Walter took on his role as foreman with gusto and soon they saw a tidy profit from the farm. Joel had Walter buy more cattle which thrilled Walter, but also exhausted him. They ended up hiring another farmhand and things settled down a bit.

Laura was also busy with all the household work, especially the bane of her existence—laundry. Although initially Mrs. Olson was to take care of the laundry, there was just too much for one person. They had to work together. Monday was laundry day and it just wore her out—the soaking, the scrubbing, the rinsing, the wringing, and then hanging it up either outside in the backyard or inside the kitchen on rainy days. When it finally dried, there was the taking it all down, ironing the pieces that needed it, and finally folding and putting it all away. Before she knew it, Monday would come around again and it started all over. Mrs. Olson continued to help out during the week, but it was exhausting trying to keep the house clean, garden tended, chickens fed, eggs gathered, cows milked –they had two cows now–and meals cooked. And of course, always the laundry.

In spite of the hard work, Laura loved having her own home with Walter by her side. They both worked hard but were so in love and happy together.

After a few months, Laura began to wonder when she would become pregnant. They made love most nights, no matter how tired they were. Usually after cleaning the kitchen—which Walter still helped her with every night—they hurried up the stairs to fall into each other's arms.

So why hadn't she become pregnant yet?

One night after about a year, Laura finally broke down after dinner and confessed to Walter how worried she was.

"What if there is something wrong with me? What if I'm barren? How will we run the farm with no sons?" she asked with tears in her eyes.

"Your pa did just fine with no sons," Walter said firmly. "Of course, I would love to have a son or daughter someday, but I will be satisfied if it is just you and me too. We have such a happy life together."

"Oh, but Walter, I want a baby," Laura cried.

Walter took her in his arms.

"I know you do. We will just keep trying and hope that God sends us a child," he said gently. "In fact, let's go upstairs and try right now."

"But the kitchen is still a mess," Laura said, looking around.

"Let's make love and then I'll come downstairs and clean up tonight. I want you to rest. Maybe you are working too hard and that's why it hasn't happened."

"I love you," she said, smiling at him with tears in her eyes.

With that, Walter picked her up and carried her upstairs.

Months turned into years. No matter how hard they tried, Laura could not get pregnant.

THIRTY-SIX

Beatrice

- 1912 -

It was a beautiful fall morning as Beatrice made her way to the millinery shop. The shop was so busy that Millicent had hired a girl named Dolores to help out with cleaning up and some of the mundane tasks. Beatrice was able to wait on customers herself now, so they could serve two ladies at once. They now had customers from all over the county.

As she entered the store, Millicent looked up from the books and smiled.

"We did well last month," she said happily. "I think it's time for you to either make more money or become a partner in the store. If you did, we could use your money to expand, maybe add on to the building. Are you interested?"

"Yes, but then we would need to hire another lady to help. We are already backlogged now," Beatrice said.

"I did meet a woman at the supply store in Kansas City last month who expressed interest in coming to work for us," Millicent told Beatrice. "I didn't mention it because I couldn't see how we could fit another workstation in here. But if we expand, it could work. What do you think? She has written to me several times, and her former employer wrote to me as well. She comes highly recommended."

"That sounds like a great plan," Beatrice answered. "Let's talk to Carl and see how we can make it an official partnership. I have some money, as you know. I was thinking of building a house, but I can wait for that."

"You wouldn't mind? I think you will get a good return for your money. But I don't want your dream of having a house to change," she said worriedly.

"I have to wait until Mamie is out of the house before I leave anyway. I don't mind waiting."

"True. Maybe if we make enough money you can still build a little house after some time. I wonder if you would permit your business partner to move in with you?" she asked.

"Well, since you wouldn't be my employer anymore I guess that could work," she chuckled. "Actually, that sounds like heaven. Imagine us being able to be together every night,"

"It would be wonderful," Millicent said, smiling tenderly at her lover.

Their employee Dolores arrived, and the ladies waited until lunch before resuming the conversation.

"Let's set up a meeting with Carl and see what he has to say," Beatrice suggested. "He can help us figure out what the business is worth and how much I should pay to become a partner."

After a fruitful meeting with Carl, the women came to an agreement. Construction started on the place a few weeks later. Beatrice spent time researching the latest designs of big city milliner shops and came up with a beautiful interior design plan for their newly expanded shop. They painted the walls a soft pink and bought new pink and gold upholstered chairs. All the lights and fixtures were gold. It was an inviting, feminine, and beautiful shop. It was dear—almost $200—but Millicent and Beatrice were hopeful that the investment in their shop would pay dividends down the road.

They closed for a month while renovating. Millicent put an ad in the St. Joseph paper to advertise their grand reopening. At the reopening party, they served refreshments and showed off the new hats Millicent had created. Beatrice hired several girls to walk around the shop, modeling the hats.

The opening was a great success, as women came from St. Joseph and beyond. Almost all the hats were sold the first day and many more were ordered.

The woman from Kansas City whom Millicent had mentioned moved to Tethertown a week after the store reopened. Her name was Florence McGill. She was a tiny woman, but full of energy and new ideas. Beatrice liked her right away.

The shop was a busy one, with the four women working from dawn to dusk six days a week. Most nights, Beatrice was too tired to spend time with Millicent at her house. In fact, a few weeks went by without them being able to spend any time alone.

After a couple of weeks, Millicent begged Beatrice to come by her house one night, but Beatrice had Mamie's wedding details and trousseau to finish. She was just too busy.

Weeks became months. Finally, Beatrice decided it was time to use some of her money to build a little two-bedroom house. It would have two entrances to give the appearance of Millicent as a renter. She bought a plot of land a bit farther out of town, so they would have lots of privacy.

Life seemed to be falling into place. Mamie was to marry in a few months and Beatrice hoped she would have made enough profit by then to build their house. Her dreams were all coming true.

One evening after leaving the shop, Beatrice realized she'd left her reticule in the back room and turned around to go back. As she unlocked the door to the dark shop, she noticed a light shining from the back room.

Someone must have left the light on, she thought and opened the door to the back room. Inside were Millicent and Florence, kissing. They both gasped, jumping apart from each other.

Beatrice cried out, put her hand over her mouth and backed away. She ran out of the shop, trying not to cry as people were about. Somehow, she made it home and ran up to her room.

In her room, she threw herself on the bed and sobbed. How could Millicent have done this? She had said she loved Beatrice! Was it all a lie?

Presently she calmed down a bit, then heard a soft knock on the door.

It was Joel. "Beatrice, may I come in?" he asked softly.

"Yes." She sniffed and sat up on the bed.

"Are you all right, my dear sister? What can I do?"

"No, I am devastated," Beatrice whispered in a strangled voice. "I caught Millicent kissing Florence. I thought she loved me!" Her eyes filled with fresh tears.

"Perhaps this was an unwanted advance—or maybe just a one-time thing? Try not to jump to conclusions," he said quietly. "It is evident that Millicent loves you. Maybe you should hear her out. She is downstairs, very distraught."

"Oh, Joel, I am so hurt. I don't even want to lay eyes on her. How could she do this to me?" she wailed.

The door opened and Millicent came in. "Can I speak to her, Joel?" she asked softly.

"Is that all right?" Joel asked Beatrice.

She turned away.

"Please hear me out," Millicent begged. "I love you, you know I do!"

Joel left the room, closing the door.

Beatrice lay on the bed, crying.

Millicent sat next to her. "I know that nothing I can say can take away the hurt you are feeling," she said softly. "I do want you to know that it was just a one-time thing. She grabbed me and kissed me. I reciprocated. I know that was very wrong of me. You came in about thirty seconds after it started. I have no excuse."

Beatrice turned her tear-stained face to look at Millicent. "How could you?"

"I don't know. I have been lonely for you as we have had very little time together, but that is no excuse. I suppose it was nice to feel young and attractive again, but it was wrong."

After a minute or two of silence, Millicent asked in a tremulous voice, "Have I ruined everything?"

Beatrice continued to look at her with tears streaming down her face. "I don't know. I need some time. I'll stay home tomorrow and think. Maybe we can meet at your house tomorrow night to talk, if I am ready."

"Yes, and I will tell Florence to leave. Although to be fair, she said she had no idea we were involved. She said we acted so professionally around each other. It is ironic that I am the one who wanted us to hide our feelings at work, and this was the result," Millicent said.

They were both silent for a moment.

"Beatrice, I am so sorry. I just can't lose you. Let me know what I can do to make it up to you!" Millicent whispered, eyes filling with tears.

"Don't do anything yet. We will talk tomorrow night," Beatrice answered and turned away.

Millicent left the room.

The next day was a miserable one for both Millicent and Beatrice. Beatrice spent time trying to concentrate on Mamie's wedding plans, but couldn't get much done. She just felt numb. What would happen to the shop if their relationship was over? Would she be able to even forgive Millicent? She had given her heart to her, but Millicent had trampled all over it. How could this have happened? Perhaps Millicent really didn't love her after all. That thought broke her heart and brought on fresh tears.

Millicent threw herself into the work at the shop, but also had a hard time concentrating. The shop felt so empty without Beatrice there. She worried that she wouldn't forgive her. What would she do? And why did she even kiss Florence anyway? She had no real excuse. Had she ruined her life? It was heartbreaking. Her life seemed pointless without Beatrice.

After Millicent cut a ribbon too short for the second time, Florence spoke up.

"Millicent, I am so sorry for what happened," she whispered after Dolores left the room. "I really had no idea you were involved with Beatrice. Please don't fire me. I promise, it will never happen again."

"That will be up to Beatrice," Millicent answered. "And it was not all your fault. For good reason, we are very circumspect around each other. I can see you didn't know. And I kissed you back." She paused. "You are right, this will never happen again. However, I would like to know why you thought I would be amenable to your advances. Most women would not."

"I'm not sure," Florence answered slowly. "It was a feeling I got around you. But I don't think that many others would know, if you are wondering. I doubt that many people would have sensed it like I did."

"Hmm. I hope you are right," Millicent said.

Millicent left work early to make a special dinner for the two of them, hoping that Beatrice would be able to forgive her. She paced around the house, worrying.

Finally, she heard Beatrice slip in the front door. The two women stood a few feet apart, looking at each other.

Millicent ran over and knelt in front of Beatrice. "Oh, my darling," she cried. "I promise this will never ever happen again. I am so heartsick. Please, please forgive me—I can't live without you!"

"Really?" Beatrice asked with tears in her eyes. "You still want to be with me?"

"Of course! I was so stupid. I can't believe I did that to us. I am so very sorry," Millicent said sobbing.

"This was partly my fault too," Beatrice said, pulling Millicent to her feet. "I have been neglecting our relationship, spending too much time on Mamie's wedding and the plans for our house."

The two women cried for a few moments, holding each other. They began kissing and then made their way to Millicent's bedroom. What followed was one of the most passionate lovemaking sessions they had ever had.

Afterwards, as they lay together, Millicent spoke up.

"We must take care of each other and put each other first. I have decided to cut down the hours of the shop and only stay open half day on Saturdays," she said. "Then we can spend more time together. If you will forgive me, that is."

"I realized today that I love you more than anything in the world. I can't even imagine life without you. It will take some time to forget, but I do forgive you," Beatrice said tearfully.

"I could never be happy again if I lost you. I wish we could be married. I love you and want only you for the rest of my life," Millicent said softly.

"I feel the same way," Beatrice replied. She was silent for a moment. "I accept your offer of marriage. Perhaps we can have our own ceremony, just the two of us, where we say vows to each other."

CHAPTER THIRTY-SIX

"What a wonderful idea!" Millicent said.

"I'd like to marry you in the garden of our new house after it is built someday. If that is alright with you," Beatrice said dreamily.

"I could make a beautiful archway of flowers for us to stand under," Millicent said. "And we can wear matching wedding hats and make new dresses. Perhaps we can invite Joel and Missy. They can be our witnesses."

"Let's do!" Beatrice said, eyes shining.

She paused for a moment. "Do you think God will bless our marriage? I know most people would say no."

"Of course, he will," exclaimed Millicent. "He sent us to each other, didn't he? I believe he wants us to be happy, don't you?

Beatrice sighed with happiness. "Yes, I do," she said.

. . .

First thing the next morning, Beatrice and Florence sat down together in the back room of the shop to talk. After Florence apologized profusely and promised never to make advances toward Millicent again, Beatrice agreed to let her stay on.

A few months later, Mamie was married in the Presbyterian Church and had a lovely lunchtime reception.

The shop continued to stay busy, but true to her word, Millicent closed on Saturday afternoons so they could spend time together.

Soon their profits were enough so that Beatrice could build their little house. The new house would be in Beatrice's name, but they decided to pool their expenses, just like any married couple.

A few months later the new house was finished and their dream of being able to move in together came true. Beatrice enjoyed decorating their new home. Millicent moved her clothing into the second bedroom, but stayed with Beatrice every night in the big bedroom. They could finally be together every night. It was heaven.

On a Saturday in early September under an archway of flowers in their garden, the two women pledged to love and care for each other for "as long as we both shall live." They said their vows in the presence of Joel and Missy. Beatrice wore a beautiful white dress, while Millicent wore a gorgeous yellow silk dress. They wore matching wedding hats, wrapped in white netting and lace with white roses on the brims.

After the wedding luncheon the two brides had prepared earlier that day, Joel and Missy hugged the happy couple and wished them well. The two women stood in the doorway, waving goodbye with their arms around each other.

"We have each other now, whatever comes," Beatrice said softly.

"Forever and ever," Millicent whispered. They smiled at each other.

THIRTY-SEVEN

Missy & Joel

-1917-

In February 1917, Americans were afraid the war in Europe would require them to fight as well.

The news from Europe seemed very far away to Missy, in Tethertown. She had her routines—helping Ezzie with her two children, visiting Laura and Walter with Joel out on the farm, visiting with Beatrice, Irene, and Mamie, taking care of her own home. Her mother had died, so she moved out of her rental house and back into her family home, which was more convenient and spacious.

Joel still visited her at night from time to time, but more out of habit than his burning desire of the past. He was now almost 50. Missy was 52. They still enjoyed each other's company, and were like a married couple in all but name. They attended events in town together, spent many evenings together, and had family dinners. Both of them were content.

Missy sometimes still longed for Billy, although it had been so many years since he died. They had been so happy together. She always regretted that he did not see Willy and Ezzie grow up, get married, and have children. How proud he would have been.

Ezzie had married a young doctor in town and now had two daughters. Willy was still in Montana and was able to finally purchase a small plot of land from a rancher to start his own cattle ranch. He had married Gretchen, a Montana girl, and they had a son they named George. Missy had never been able to figure out how to make the long trek out there, but wished that she could. She was not sure she had the courage to travel that far alone.

One night while they were lying in Missy's bed, Joel asked her if she missed Willy.

"Of course, I do!" she exclaimed. "What a question. I have never even met my daughter-in-law or my grandson."

"What if we took the train out there to see him?" Joel asked. "I would love to see Montana, as well as Willy. I have always loved him like a son."

"I know you have," Missy said softly. "But it is so far. We would be gone for a long time. Would you be able to leave for so long?"

"I think so. The farm is in good hands with Walter. My other responsibilities in town can be put off. What if we went in April?" he asked.

"Oh, do you think it would be possible?" she asked in a shaky voice. "I would love to see him again!"

"Let me look into the arrangements tomorrow. We can leave at the beginning of April, if that works for you," he said. "But it will most likely take a few weeks to get there. It is far away. It could be a hard trip."

"I don't care," she said. "I want to go. Oh, Joel, you are so good to me!"

Joel looked into the trip the next day. It would take close to two weeks to get to Helena. It was also expensive. When he went out to the farm to see Laura that week, they talked it over.

"Oh, Pa, that sounds like a hard trip—but so exciting," Laura said. "I bet it's more like the Wild West out there. You've always wanted to see Montana."

"I agree," said Walter. "It's about time for you to have an adventure. We will be fine."

"Oh, I know you will," Joel said. "I'm not worried about the farm. But, it is a long way to go."

"It would be such a good thing to do for Missy," Laura said. "I know she longs to see Willy again, and meet her grandson and Gretchen. I think you should do it."

Just mentioning Missy's grandson made Laura feel sad. Yes, Walter and Laura had a happy life together and continued to have an intense passion between them. But still—no baby. She was beginning to realize that they might never have a child.

Mamie also seemed unable to get pregnant. Only Irene was lucky in that regard. Her first child was due in June.

. . .

After speaking to Irene and Mamie, Joel went to purchase tickets to leave on April 7th from St. Joseph to Helena, Montana.

On April 6th as they were preparing to leave for St. Joseph to start their trip, the country got terrible news. President Wilson asked Congress to declare war on Germany. Reluctantly, Joel and Missy decided to put off their trip.

"Most certainly Congress will vote to conscript soldiers," Joel told Missy. "That could mean Willy, Walter, and all our girls' husbands will go off to war. Perhaps we should send a telegram to see if Gretchen and little George want to come here? I would think life in Montana without her husband would be hard. And Gretchen has no family there, does she?"

"No, she does not," Missy said. "Her parents died just last year in a fire. Perhaps Willy can sell his cattle and bring them here before he goes."

"You can offer and let them think it over," Joel suggested. "We will send them a telegram. I can change our tickets to have them ride the train here instead."

"Oh, could you?" Missy asked. "I don't know if they could afford the train fare otherwise."

A month later, Willy made the decision to enlist before he could be conscripted. He then decided to sell his cattle and bring his family to Tethertown for the duration of the war. It was bittersweet for Missy: she would see her son and meet his family, but then he would go off to war.

All of Joel's sons-in-law were preparing to leave for war as well. Joel would move out to the farm to run it as best as he could—with some farmhands who were too young to go to war, he hoped. Sooner or later, many of the men between eighteen and thirty-one would be conscripted or enlist.

Walter was not going to wait to be conscripted, as he was of German descent. People in town had been suspicious of Walter and his brothers since the start of the Great War in Europe, and the feeling had only escalated since the sinking of so many American ships. Walter and his brothers knew that if they were not to be harassed, they must join the war effort as soldiers immediately. They were due to travel to Fort Sheridan soon.

Laura and Joel decided to have a big family dinner in the backyard of the farmhouse the evening before Walter and his brothers were to leave. All of the ladies, including Walter's mother, had worked all week baking pies and cakes and then cooking all day to put on the special dinner. Walter's brothers Hans and Friedrich were to join the party as well.

Just as everyone had gathered and were sitting down to dinner, they heard a wagon pull up outside.

"Now, who could that be?" Joel asked, mystified.

"I'll go check," said Walter and he went to the door.

Willy and his family came around the corner.

The family erupted with joy. Missy burst into tears and hugged her son, daughter-in-law, and two-year-old grandson George. The family had a feast while hearing about Montana and the two-week train trip to Missouri.

"The train was full of young men signing up to go join the fight in France," Willy told the family. "Many of those boys were only eighteen. I decided I might as well do the same and not wait to be called."

"I was thinking the same thing," Mamie's husband said. "Walter and his brothers, Hans and Friedrich, are leaving tomorrow. They can get there ahead and write to us so we know what to expect."

"I imagine it is a lot of hard work, tons of drilling, and getting into marching shape, all while eating terrible food." Walter said with a smile. "I'll be happy to write and tell you all about it."

"I'd go today if Irene wasn't due to have our baby in June," Carl said. "As soon as that baby is born, I will join you all."

"Now Carl, don't be in such a hurry to go," Beatrice said. "You will want to get to know your little one a bit before you run off."

"Well, we'll see," he replied. "If I am conscripted, I will have no choice."

Walter, who was usually a very shy man, stood up to speak. "I want to thank everyone here for this dinner and all the support you have given Laura and me. I know I leave her in good hands, that you all will watch over each other and help each other. I hope you will all watch over my Mother as well. Laura will especially need your help—isn't that right, my dear?"

Laura blushed. "Yes," she said. "I am going to have a little one in October."

Again, the family erupted with joy.

After everyone settled down, Irene whispered to Laura. "October? But that's only five months away! Why didn't you tell me?"

"Believe me, I am as surprised as you are. I was feeling ill but had no other symptoms. I went to see the doctor yesterday and he gave me the happy news." Laura whispered. "I still can't believe it!"

"Oh, but that means Walter will be gone!" Mamie said aloud.

Walter grimaced. "I know. I feel terrible about that. After all these years and just when I enlist, wouldn't you know," Walter said, shaking his head. "I'm still in shock."

"We will send many letters telling you about your child, my dear," Beatrice promised Walter.

"I'll draw portraits of your baby and send them to you as well," Millicent added.

"Oh, I am so happy to be a grandmother at last!" Walter's mother cried.

Everyone cheered again.

THIRTY-EIGHT

Walter & Laura

After everyone left and Joel had gone to bed, Walter took Laura's hand and led her upstairs.

"I want to explore every inch of your body," he whispered. "Let me undress you and let's give each other a night to remember."

"Oh, Walter, I could never forget these moments. I will treasure them when you are gone," Laura said, her eyes filling.

Walter undressed her slowly and kissed her all over gently. He laid her on the bed, spread her legs and began to gently stroke her thighs, softly moving to her labia. Soon, he began gently blowing on and around her vagina, slowly getting his mouth closer and closer. He then began exploring her with his mouth. He continued until she begged him to enter her.

Walter used all his willpower to slowly enter her. They moved together. Both began to moan, and finally climaxed.

As they lay in each other's arms afterwards, Laura tried to stay positive but soon began to weep.

Are you alright?" Walter asked, looking at her face in the candlelight. "What is wrong? Was that too much for you? Did it hurt?"

"Oh no. Nothing like that," she replied in a choking voice. "It was wonderful. But what shall I do without you? I'm so happy that we are finally having our baby. I wish so much that you could be here."

"Let's not think about that now," Walter said softly. "Instead let's hold each other and make love again in a while, just like on our wedding night."

The couple spent most of the night talking and making love. The next morning, they were exhausted, but Walter had to leave for the train.

He leaned over and kissed Laura as long as he could. "I must go," he whispered. "But you must go back to sleep. You need your rest, with the baby coming. I love you, my dear. Please always remember that, no matter what happens."

"I will think of you every moment. Be careful and come back to me," Laura said, crying.

With one more kiss, Walter stood and got up to leave. When he reached the door, he turned to look at his wife once more. She had tears in her eyes, but was smiling at him bravely.

I will keep this picture in my head, he promised himself. *Laura at dawn, with her tousled hair, tired from making love, carrying my child, and more beautiful than ever.*

Then he walked out of the door.

. . .

The days after Walter left moved slowly for Laura. He had promised to write often, but he was, and had always been, a man of few words. He sent a short letter at least once a week, with messages to relay to her brothers-in-law about items to bring to boot camp as well as brief descriptions of life at the Fort. Walter did not complain. He said little about his feelings, except that he missed her and hoped she was well.

Willy, along with Mamie's husband Jim, left soon after Walter did. Carl waited for Irene to have their baby. Their baby boy finally arrived on a warm June morning. He left for the fort a week later.

By September of 1917, Laura was big with child and missing Walter very much. He had arrived in France and was due to leave for the trenches shortly. Willy, Jim, and Carl would be shipped off to France soon as well.

The women got together often to console each other. Laura decided to stay in town the last month so she would be close to her sisters and to the midwife. She kept busy knitting baby clothes, visiting friends, her sisters, Beatrice, and her new cousin Gretchen at Missy's house.

October came with an early frost. Laura knew that Walter was now in the trenches. He wrote little, except to say that he was fine and missing her. Between worrying about her upcoming labor and Walter, Laura had a hard time sleeping.

Finally in mid-October, she woke up in the middle of the night realizing that her water had broken and that she had started labor. Joel happened to be staying in the town house that night, so he went to get her sisters, Beatrice, and the midwife.

After many hours of pain, Laura finally gave birth to a tiny girl whom she named Mary Kathleen. They had decided on baby names before he left—Mary after her sister and Kathleen because it was Laura's favorite name. Looking in her baby's eyes, she felt a fierce protectiveness and an overpowering joy. At the same time, she felt a deep sadness that Walter was not there. She teared up, realizing that he might never even meet his daughter.

Just as promised, Millicent came by and drew several portraits of Laura holding the baby and some just of Mary Kathleen. Laura dictated a letter to Beatrice as she was too tired to write.

My dearest husband,

Your baby girl was born today. Mary Kathleen weighed 6 lbs. and came out yelling! She is healthy and is already nursing. She is now sleeping in the cradle your father made for you when you were a baby. Your mother sent it to me this week. Somehow, it makes me feel closer to you.

Oh Walter, she is so beautiful. She has your dark hair and dark eyes. She took a while to get here, but the midwife assured me that this was a fast birth. It didn't seem that way to me, but I got through it all right.

How I wish you were here to meet your baby girl and to kiss us both. I will end this now so we can mail it right away, but I want you to know we are both well and that we hope and pray to see you soon. Please take care of yourself, my darling.

With love from your Laura and little Mary Kathleen

A week later, Walter received the letter during the evening mess. The men celebrated with him by confiscating some of the sergeant's rum. Walter had too much to drink and when the sergeant walked up, he could smell the rum.

"What's this, soldier?" he asked in a harsh tone. "Are you drunk? Did you get into my rum?"

"Hey Sarge, it was my idea," one of Walter's fellow soldiers said. "Walter just found out his wife had a baby girl. We were celebrating!"

"You shut up, Private Marsh," the sergeant growled. "That's all we need—another Goddamn Hun in this world!"

Walter looked up with murder in his eyes. Before he could say anything, his friend Ben pushed him down on the ground.

"Look, Sarge. I will take the punishment. I drank, too. Let's not ruin this happy news for Walter."

"Do you think I give a shit about Walter?" The sergeant barked. He turned to Walter. "Private Bauer, you will have Field Punishment number one for a week. That is all. And the rest of you shut up or you'll join him."

So, for a week, Walter was subjected to Field Punishment No. 1, which the men had nicknamed "crucifixion." He performed hard labor for two hours each day while a heavy wheel was attached to his back.

"I'm real sorry," his buddy Ben said to him after the first day. "I never should have taken that rum."

"It's all right," Walter said. "I like having work to do, even though it is disgusting cleaning the latrines. The wheel just makes my muscles stronger, so I don't really mind."

"That's true," Ben said.

"But please don't tell Sarge I said so," he added. "He will probably give me another week if he finds out."

It was hell in that trench. If it wasn't muddy from the rain, it was dusty. It smelled terrible. Everyone and everything was filthy. Living there was a miserable existence.

Although the Germans were retreating, they still managed to bombard them with shells and even gassed some of the Americans ahead of them. The thought of being gassed horrified Walter. He had heard of men going blind or dying in agony.

Another problem was the wolves. They had been displaced by all the damage to the forests and their hunting grounds. To survive, they learned to roam the trenches, stealing food and—even worse—killing sleeping soldiers. It got so bad that one day the Germans, French, and Americans called a ceasefire to hunt them. Walter and his brothers had hunted and killed a wolf on their farm in Kentucky years ago, but these wolves were much bigger and completely fearless. They were terrifying.

The rats were a nightmare as well. One could never be rid of them, and there seemed to be more of them every day. One of Walter's fellow soldiers grew ill and, while he was sleeping, the rats began to gnaw on his face and hands. It was enough to give the bravest man nightmares—or keep him awake at night in terror as rats crawled on them while they slept. Some men got used to it and ignored them, but Walter never could. He didn't get much sleep.

But with all the hell he was going through with wolves, rats, lice, poor rations, and lack of sleep, Walter's biggest worry was Laura. What would happen to her if he died? By this time, he figured that he most likely would die. Two of his buddies had been blown to bits the week before, right next to him. He felt such sorrow that he would never meet his daughter or hold Laura in his arms again.

On top of that, many of the newer soldiers recognized that he was of German descent and constantly harassed him. He had some buddies like Ben who tried to stand up for him, but it was a losing battle.

Walter did not want Laura to know any of that, so he wrote to her very little, sometimes relaying a funny story about a friend or a moment of quiet and peace. And those moments exsisted, although few and far between.

One morning he woke early and beyond the blackened landscape, he saw a beautiful bright pink and orange sunrise. Two doves flew overhead, which seemed a miracle to him as he had not seen any birds—other than vultures—since he had entered the trenches many months earlier. He felt sure that it was a message from God, telling him there would be a better day coming.

In that moment, he took heart. He described the scene to Laura in his letter home.

Reading Walter's account of the sunrise, Laura's eyes filled with tears. She prayed so hard for her husband every day, and now God had sent him a ray of hope. Through that letter, she began to feel hopeful as well.

A week later, a shell exploded near Walter, severely injuring his leg. The doctors performed an emergency operation. They were able to save the leg, but Walter would be unable to return to active duty.

"If you stay free from infection, you should be able to walk soon," the doctor told Walter. "But you are not fit for fighting in the trenches anymore. Perhaps you can help with translating—I understand you speak German."

"Yes, sir," Walter replied. "I offered to help with translating before, but they turned me down."

"Well, we could use your help now," the doctor replied. "Several of our translators were killed in the latest shelling. I'll let the General know."

THIRTY-NINE

Walter & Laura

Somehow Walter survived and did not get an infection, although he would have a limp the rest of his life. Walter knew he had been spared—he had gotten word that his entire platoon had been gassed a few days after his injury, including his friend Ben.

Walter was now in a hospital tent a mile or so from the trenches. He realized he was lucky to have gotten injured or he would have been gassed too, but the survivor's guilt was debilitating. Many mornings he could barely make himself get out of bed. For weeks he had nightmares, seeing his friends choking and dying. He would wake up in a cold sweat and then the guilt would hit him.

He began to feel like a black cloud was hanging over him. It reminded him of when his father died, and they had to leave their home. He remembered that terrible feeling, Walter was despondent. He had a hard time speaking to anyone, instead he just stared off into space and was silent.

Walter stopped eating. Food just didn't taste good anymore and he had no appetite. He became so thin that the doctor threatened to move him to the "mental ward" if he didn't start eating. Walter had heard terrible stories about that place, where men were chained to their beds, screaming and moaning all day long. So, he started to choke down enough food to get by.

The general put him to work translating, which was a welcome diversion. When he was busy translating, he could block out the thoughts of his friends dying. He continued to receive letters from Laura and his mother, but was too exhausted and depressed to write back.

After a while, the letters from Laura and his mother kept asking if he was alright. He could tell they were really starting to worry. But somehow, he just couldn't think of what to write to them. So, he didn't.

When he received word that his brother Fredrich had been killed by a sniper, he sunk even lower. Then he got a letter from his grieving mother, begging him to write and tell him he was still alive. That desperate letter helped him to realize that he was being selfish. He finally sat down to write his mother. She needed him to reassure her. The same day he wrote to Laura and explained to her about his melancholy but assured her that he was feeling better—even though the "black cloud" still hung over him every day. He continued to write to Laura and his mother once a week. Somehow, he found that sharing his thoughts did make him feel a bit better.

But really, it was the work of translating that helped him to recover. After a month or two, he even heard himself laughing one day. He spent the rest of the war far from the front lines, listening to and translating German radio messages.

Meanwhile, the Spanish flu was raging everywhere. In Tethertown, both Beatrice and Millicent took ill. Mamie was the only one without a child, so she went to nurse them. Unfortunately, Mamie came down with the flu as well. After a few harrowing weeks filled with fear, the three women recovered. They were lucky.

Many in Tethertown did not survive. Walter's Aunt Gerta died. Somehow his mother never got sick, even though she nursed his aunt. Irene fell ill and went to Joel's house to keep her children from getting sick. She was nursed by Mrs. Ware who also contracted the flu. Mrs. Ware died two weeks later. This was hard on Laura, Irene, and Mamie. After all, she had been with them their whole lives.

Then Missy took ill. It was touch and go for a while. Joel never left her side. He spent many nights sitting with her, begging her not to leave him.

Happily, Missy recovered. Somehow, Joel, Laura, and Mary Kathleen never became ill. The rest of Missy's family never got sick either. The doctor could not explain why some people got it while others did not. This flu was a mystery.

On the front lines in France, many men died of the flu. Willy came down with it and died. They waited until Missy was fully recovered before they told her, fearing that she would relapse.

Walter's brother Hans also took ill and died. Walter was spared and did not get sick. But he continued to feel blue, especially after hearing the news about Hans. Both of his brothers were gone. He began to have nightmares that he returned home, and his mother, Laura, and the baby were all dead. He would wake up in a cold sweat. He knew that if that happened, he would not want to live anymore.

Why have I been spared? he would wonder at night.

But then he would tell himself he needed to be alive for Laura, his mother, and especially for his baby.

Finally, in November 1918, fighting on the Western Front ceased. The victory was bittersweet for Walter. He had lost so many friends. He was sent home in December. Laura was to meet him at the St. Joseph train station on a cold Tuesday afternoon.

Laura wanted to look her best for Walter, so she dressed carefully in her finest clothing. She wore a dark blue walking suit and her new tailored hat, designed by Millicent. Happily, whalebone corsets were out. Women wore girdles instead, which were much more comfortable. Skirts and dresses were shorter—to the calf—with ankle length fuller underskirts. What would Walter think? Would he be scandalized by her silhouette and shorter skirt?

As Laura stood on the platform waiting for Walter's train, she felt anxious. He had been gone almost 19 months. What if he had changed? Would he still be sad and morose? Would he still love her? Would he still want her?

Her brother-in-law Carl had come home the month before and was in poor shape. The doctor called it shell shock. Carl just cried all day, refusing to leave the bedroom. Irene was having a hard time taking care of both Carl and their young son.

Laura was not foolish enough to believe that Walter had been spared all the horrors of the trenches, even though he had never told her much about them. She worried that he too would have shell shock when he returned home.

When the train pulled up and soldiers began to disembark, Laura looked around anxiously. Would she even recognize her husband?

She heard a shout.

"Laura!"

She turned around and saw her darling Walter limping toward her. She flew into his arms and began to cry. "Oh, Walter, oh my dear!"

Walter too was holding onto her for dear life and hoarsely crying out. They kissed and cried and kissed again. Then slowly they made their way to Joel and the waiting car.

All around them, Laura could see similar tableaux playing out. They walked near the area where the severely injured were being taken off the train. Laura saw so many brave faces of mothers, wives, and sweethearts trying to smile, even though it must be shocking to see the men they loved in such bad shape.

She also noticed the faces of the injured soldiers. These were men who knew how different their lives would be now without legs, or an arm, or sight. They were also putting on a brave face. Some would lead productive lives, some would not. They knew they would be a burden on their families. The war had wrecked their futures.

Walter was deeply affected when looking at the injured soldiers. "Such a waste, so many lives ruined," he said quietly, despair etched on his face.

"How lucky we are to have you home and healthy," Laura said after they passed by. "Does your leg hurt? Oh Walter, you are so thin. But I am so grateful you are home."

Walter stopped in his tracks, his face turning white.

"Where is Mary Kathleen?" he asked. "Is she well? I thought she would be here."

"No, it's so cold out and I didn't want her to get a chill," Laura said. "She is at the house in town. You will see her as soon as we get there, I promise."

"That makes sense," Walter said, looking relieved. "I think I am so used to bad things happening, it will take me time to adjust to normal life again."

"Carl is really suffering," Laura said. "He has terrible dreams at night and sits around all day crying, shut up in his room. Irene does not know what to do. The doctor says it is shell shock. Have you heard of that?"

"Oh yes," Walter said grimly. "Some of the men had it bad and couldn't do anything in the trenches but just cower. A few of them even took their own lives. Some ran away and were caught and then shot. People say it was because they were cowards, but I think it was because they saw too much. They were frightened out of their wits, and for good reason."

"Oh, Walter," was all Laura could say.

They were silent for a moment.

"So many terrible things happened. I don't know how anyone could say they were cowards." Walter began to get angry. "Are folks saying bad things about Carl?"

"I wouldn't be surprised, " Laura said sadly. "You know how folks are."

"I'll go spend some time with him," Walter said thoughtfully. "We were close friends before and maybe I could help him. We're both soldiers, after all."

"Oh, would you? I know Irene would be so grateful. The doctor suggested sending him to an asylum, but she doesn't want to do that."

The couple arrived at the place where Joel was parked. Joel had recently bought a Ford Model TT truck for the farm. He was anxious to show Walter, who had always hoped to have a truck on the farm someday.

He jumped out and shook Walter's hand. "How are you, son? " he asked. "We are so glad you are home. Your mother is at the house, and you will see her and your feisty one-year-old daughter very soon."

"Thank you, sir, for taking care of my family while I was away. I sure like your new truck."

"Well, they're my family too—just as you are," Joel said, smiling at him. "Just wait till we get to the farm and you see how much easier farm work is with a truck. But first we'll need to go to the town house. Everyone is so anxious to see you, especially your mother."

The rest of the day was one of the happiest Laura had ever had. She had her beloved back, he finally met his daughter, and her family was around her. She kept touching Walter to make sure he was real.

At times she would catch him staring, with a strange blank look on his face. But when she asked him if he was ok, he would smile and say he was fine. She hoped it was true.

Walter's mother was happy to see him, but cried bitter tears thinking of the sons she would never see again. While clinging to Walter, she cried, "I want my sons" over and over again.

Walter kept saying to her, "Mother, I am here." But even being with Walter could not make up for the loss of her two oldest sons. It was heartbreaking.

By the end of dinner, Walter's mother was exhausted. Walter took her home and sat with her until she went to sleep.

"I think seeing me brought it back to her that she would never see my brothers again," he told Laura later. "With my aunt gone, I worry about her in that house alone."

"I agree. Perhaps she needs to come live with us at the farm," Laura suggested. "We can take care of her there. It might help her to be around Mary Kathleen."

"Could we?" Walter asked. "I have been so worried about her, especially when I think about her alone in town and us so far away, out at the farm."

"Of course," Laura said. "Now I have put Mary Kathleen to bed, and it is our turn for bed. Can you come with me to our room, my darling?"

Once they closed the door, Walter turned on the gaslight, then took her hand and asked her to sit down.

"I am worried that I will not be able to make love anymore," he confessed. "My leg wound was very close to my groin. The doctor said I might have difficulties."

"Oh, poof," Laura said. "What does the doctor know? I don't believe it. Why look, you are already ready."

Laura began to unbutton her dress. "I think we will be fine." She slowly finished undressing in front of him.

"Oh, how I have dreamed of this," he sighed. "Just look at you. You are so beautiful."

"But my body is different now, I have had a baby. I was worried you would be disappointed in me," she confessed.

"Oh, never, ever could that happen," he said, burying himself in her breasts.

They fell onto the bed, kissing and stroking one another. Laura finally saw his wound. It had indeed been dangerously close to the groin. The scar was very red—almost purple—and looked as if it was sore to the touch. But Walter swore it didn't hurt much anymore.

"Are you sure this is ok?" Laura asked while gently tracing his wound with her fingertips.

"It's better than ok," Walter said grinning at her. He kissed her hard and climbed on top of her, climaxing soon after he entered her.

"I'm sorry, I guess I was too eager," he said afterwards.

"Don't worry, we have the rest of our lives for leisurely lovemaking now. I love it that you were hungry for me, just like I was for you."

"I dreamed of this moment so many times. Lying here beside you, naked in my arms," he said softly.

"I am so happy," Laura whispered. The couple fell asleep, entwined in each other's arms.

At dawn, Walter began gently kissing her naked body until she awakened. He sucked, kissed, and gently stroked her until she begged to have him inside her again. He entered her much slower this time. The two came together, rocking and moaning until they both climaxed.

"Well, that doctor was wrong to worry about your virility," Laura said breathlessly after they finished. "I would say you are even better than before!"

Walter was happy to be with Laura's family but longed to be out at the farm. He knew that working outdoors was the best cure for his melancholy.

After visiting Carl a few times and getting little response, he decided to give him some more time to recover. A week later, they packed up his mother and the little family moved back out to the farm in the new Model TT truck. The truck would make his work much easier, especially with his leg. It would be at least a year before his leg was totally healed.

As Walter stood in the field with his mother that day, he made a promise to her, "We will build a new life out here and give you grandsons. They will never take the place of my brothers, but I hope they will console you."

"Oh no, I want granddaughters now," she answered. "I have my son."

Walter was so grateful. He had survived, his family was healthy, and the farm was prospering. He was starting to feel like himself again. God was good.

FORTY

It was a good winter for the Watson family. To their utter joy, Laura was pregnant again. The farm was doing well. All the men who had fought in the war and survived were home, although Carl was still suffering from shell shock. He was slowly improving but there were still days he couldn't leave his room and loud, everyday noises continued to scare him. Walter visited with him at least once a week and he was able to have a conversation with him some days. Carl confessed that he still had such bad nightmares that he was afraid to go to sleep some nights.

One day, Walter asked him if he wanted to talk about the war. Carl turned white and just shook his head. It was many years before he could speak of it with Walter.

Walter thanked God that he had been able to recover from the horrors of war. He still had some tough nights but, on the whole, was feeling more and more like his old self every day. Hard work on the farm was the best medicine. He hoped Carl would be able to recover someday too.

After a few months, Carl tried to go back to work, but he couldn't tolerate being away from home. Carl would never practice law again, the war had taken too much of a toll on his nerves.

Missy was also struggling, losing her son Willy had been devastating. Willy's wife Gretchen and her son George had stayed on with her, as they had no source of income now. Having little George around helped the women from sinking into despair. Missy was grateful to Gretchen for staying, but she missed her nights with Joel, especially in her grief.

Spring finally arrived and the family decided to have a big picnic out at the lake. All of the daughters and daughters-in-law put together a big spread. There was ham, fried chicken, deviled eggs, potato salad, coleslaw, biscuits, cookies, pies, lemonade, and beer. The women sat on blankets chatting, while the men threw a baseball to each other. The children ran around the picnic area, shouting and laughing. Little Mary Kathleen crawled after them, looking as if she wanted to join in. There was a soft wind and a blue sky, it was a beautiful day.

After they all ate, Missy and Joel went for a walk. As they strolled beside the lake, the two reminisced about the many times they would sneak off to make love in the tall grass. They smiled and laughed together.

Joel stopped under a budding apple tree and kissed Missy passionately.

"I have missed your touch, especially during my sad and lonely nights," Missy said. "So many nights I think of Willy and want your arms around me. But I can't scandalize Gretchen by staying with you anymore."

"Why don't we start having dinner at my house in town?" he suggested. "Then we could have some time alone together."

"Yes," she said. "We could do that. But I would still be lonely at night."

"Or perhaps we will finally marry and you will move into the house with me," Joel said, smiling. "Missy, we have loved each other for such a long time. I think we need each other now."

Joel knelt down and took out a big diamond ring. "I bought this in St. Joseph a year ago," Joel confessed. "But then you got sick, and Walter got injured, and Willy died. So, I have waited. But I think it is now time, my love. Missy, will you please marry me?"

"Oh, Joel!" Missy cried. "Do you mean it?"

"I mean it only if you say yes. But hurry up, because my knee hurts."

"Yes—oh, yes!" she cried and pulled him to his feet. "But what will the girls think?"

"Oh, they'll be thrilled. Mamie suggested I do it today so we can all celebrate."

"Wait—you told her? Who else knows?"

"Just Laura, Irene, Mamie, Beatrice, Millicent, and Gretchen. Oh, and the husbands probably know, too."

"What if I had said no?" she asked, amazed.

"Then your whole family would bully you into saying yes. We all want this. But especially me," he said, embracing her,

"I think Billy, Belle, and Willy would be happy too," said Missy.

The two made their way back to the family, who were waiting anxiously. When Joel and Missy walked into the clearing and smiled, a big cheer went up. Even Carl smiled a little.

Two months later, in the same church where Missy had married Billy, Joel and Missy became husband and wife. As they walked out of the church, half of the town was outside, cheering and throwing rice.

That night as they got into bed, Missy sighed. "I was always afraid if we married, our sex life wouldn't be as exciting," she said.

"Let's see what we can do about that," Joel said smiling, and took her into his arms.

Connect

www.maryhopkinsmoore.com

@maryhopkinsmoore

@maryhopkinsmoore

mary@maryhopkinsmoore.com

Acknowledgements

It had been a lifelong dream of mine to write a book, but I seemed to lack the time and headspace to do so. I was too busy—raising kids, working at a job I loved, and letting life keep me busy.

When I finally became a retiree, I surprised myself. I almost immediately started working on this book. I didn't plan it—it seemed to just happen. Once I settled on my subject (Joel) the writing came quickly. I had to stop and do some research at times but still, my first draft was finished after about two months.

Then came the editing, which took over a year. I found a great editor in Clair Lamb through one of my favorite authors Jonathan Cullen. Clair helped me immensely, not just with grammar and sentence structure, but also by encouraging me to go into more depth. She is an amazing editor.

Some of my family members added suggestions—my husband Tom, daughter Carolyn, and daughter-in-law Kira were all very helpful. But the most help of all came from my niece KS Revivo.

KS not only helped me edit, but also created the cover and designed the book. She is a busy working mom of two girls but generously gave her precious time to this book, and to me. I am beyond grateful to her.

So many people encouraged me—friends, co-workers from the Hyde School, and of course, my family of origin. My parents raised all six of us to work hard and to never give up. I was so lucky to have them as parents, as well as having siblings who love me unconditionally.

But my most heartfelt gratitude is to my immediate family—my husband Tom, children Patrick, Bobby, Joey, and Carolyn, daughters-in-law Kira, Alondra and Patty and grandchildren Wyatt, Cecilia, Natalie, and Emma. My family inspires me to do my best and keep reaching for the stars. They always believe in me and make me feel so loved every day.

Finally, thank you to my readers, whoever you are.